PRAISE FOR MIRACLES HAPPEN WHEN WOMEN PRAY

Jesus taught that when you find Kingdom treasure, sell everything to get the field where it's buried. Having ministered with Bobbye Byerly for years, I can tell you that she is a woman of God full of Kingdom treasures. In *Miracles Happen When Women Pray,* you'll discover just how wealthy with Christ God has made her as she bravely lays out her whole life before you. Buy it. Dig into it. Be thoroughly enriched by it. Discover what miracles can look like.

David Bryant

Chairman, America's National Prayer Committee
President, Concerts of Prayer International

This book will not only inspire and encourage readers to pursue God for intimacy with Himself, but to enter into greater heights and depths of the priceless and rewarding ministry of intercession. Bobbye shares her heart and experiences with clarity and conviction.

Joy Dawson

International Bible teacher and author

Women were created to birth life, not only physically, but spiritually as well. In fact, let me add myself to the great list of miracles in Bobbye Byerly's inspiring book. My mother prayed me into the kingdom of God. Perhaps there is nothing Satan fears more than a nation of praying women.

Francis Frangipane

Author, *Holiness, Truth and the Presence of God*
Pastor, River of Life Ministries
Cedar Rapids, Iowa

Inspirational! Easy to read! An incredible story of one woman's courageous and lifelong pursuit of God in the adventure of prayer—a life filled with the joy of intimacy, simple trust, exciting miracles and global purpose straight from the Father's heart. This book is for anyone who truly desires a closer and more fulfilling walk with God!

Barbara James

Codirector, World Intercession Network (WIN)

Bobbye Byerly has endured testing to become a testimony! Her book *Miracles Happen When Women Pray* will impart that same overcoming spirit into your life. I have been privileged to be in the prayer room beside this wonderful woman of God; I know of very few people who walk in the disciplined love of God like she does. This book will cause an impartation to come into your life and revolutionize the way you pray.

Dr. Chuck Pierce

Vice President, Global Harvest Outreach
President, Glory of Zion International

Bobbye Byerly's testimony is a beautiful example of the powerful influence one woman has when she says yes to God and loses her life in Him. She, like Mary of Bethany, has chosen the "better part" and she continues to teach and inspire us all to do the same. To quote Bobbye, "When we walk in holy intimacy with Him, miracles will happen."

Marilyn Quirk

Magnificat, A Ministry to Catholic Women

Bobbye Byerly is a woman who daily experiences the power of prayer. But before she had ever heard the term "intercessory prayer" she responded to God's call to lift up every concern to His loving heart. As a result she began to experience an ever-increasing intimacy with Him and His miracle-working power. God can do the same thing in your life when you allow Him to be your greatest joy and to love the world through your prayers.

Dutch Sheets

Pastor, Springs Harvest Fellowship
Colorado Springs, Colorado

Bobbye Byerly is a woman who has a heart for God and His purposes. This book, a testimony of what God has done in her life, will bless and encourage you and make you hunger to know God in the same intimate way as this seasoned intercessor. I have spent many prayer times with her over the years and I can attest to incredible answers that resulted from her prayers.

Quin Sherrer

Author, *Praying Prodigals Home*

I love Bobbye Byerly! She is a godly woman who displays the sweet fragrance of God. I wholly recommend her book *Miracles Happen When Women Pray*, in which Bobbye shares with us the experiences of her life—both the traumatic and powerful! You will be stirred and challenged with her faith, her passion and anointing. Enjoy the charisma of my wonderful friend.

Alice Smith

Executive Director, U.S. Prayer Center
Houston, Texas

If you believe prayer is powerful, you'll love this book. Bobbye Byerly's eventful life as a seasoned intercessor opens exciting new vistas for seeing how God's hand moves in response to our prayers. This is a heartwarming book!

C. Peter Wagner

Chancellor, Wagner Leadership Institute

BOBBYE BYERLY

Miracles Happen

WHEN WOMEN PRAY

From Gospel Light
Ventura, California, U.S.A.

Published by Regal Books
From Gospel Light
Ventura, California, U.S.A.
Printed in the U.S.A.

Regal Books is a ministry of Gospel Light, an evangelical Christian publisher dedicated to serving the local church. We believe God's vision for Gospel Light is to provide church leaders with biblical, user-friendly materials that will help them evangelize, disciple and minister to children, youth and families.

It is our prayer that this Regal book will help you discover biblical truth for your own life and help you meet the needs of others. May God richly bless you.

For a free catalog of resources from Regal Books/Gospel Light, please call your Christian supplier or contact us at 1-800-4-GOSPEL *or* www.regalbooks.com.

Cover and Interior Design by Robert Williams
Edited by Linda Cagnetti and Rose Decaen

LIBRARY OF CONGRESS CATALOGING-IN-PUBLICATION DATA
Byerly, Bobbye, 1932-
Miracles happen when women pray / Bobbye Byerly.
p. cm.
ISBN 0-8307-2646-2
1. Christian women—Religious life. 2. Intercessory prayer—Christianity.
3. Miracles. I. Title.
BV4527 .B94 2002
248.3'2—dc21 2001006386

1 2 3 4 5 6 7 8 9 10 11 12 13 14 15 / 09 08 07 06 05 04 03 02

Rights for publishing this book in other languages are contracted by Gospel Light Worldwide, the international nonprofit ministry of Gospel Light. Gospel Light Worldwide also provides publishing and technical assistance to international publishers dedicated to producing Sunday School and Vacation Bible School curricula and books in the languages of the world. For additional information, visit www.gospellightworldwide.org; write to Gospel Light Worldwide, P.O. Box 3875, Ventura, CA 93006; or send an e-mail to info@gospellightworldwide.org.

I DEDICATE THIS BOOK

TO MY LORD, JESUS CHRIST,

AND THE FAMILY HE HAS

GIVEN ME HERE ON EARTH.

PRAISE HIS NAME,

FOREVER.

Contents

Acknowledgments

Hallelujah! I want to express publicly before His people my heartfelt thanks to God for His mighty miracles in my life. All who are thankful should ponder these with me. His miracles are a demonstration of His honor, majesty and eternal goodness. Who can forget His deeds of mercy and grace?

I thank the Lord for the graciousness and encouragement Regal books has offered me in bringing forth my first book.

I want to express my deep love and heartfelt thanks to my covenant lover and partner in life, Jim, my husband for over 50 glorious years. And many thanks go to our three sons and their wives who have kept urging me to write a book sharing the goodness of God's love. Because of their great outpouring of love and confidence, I have completed this story of Jesus' love and work in my life.

Now, I also owe a deep debt of thanks to Quin Sherrer, who prayed with me and shared with me, showing me that there were books within me that needed to come forth. Your confidence, Quin, helped me throughout this two-year process.

Also, I cannot forget the support of my dear friends, Barbara James, Mickie Winborn, Judy Ball, Marilyn Quirk, Kay and Paul LaPeyre and Betsy and Hank Teuton, who kept believing in me and encouraging me to finish the task.

Thanks to my sister, Jeanne, and my brother, Richard, who have both supported me with their great expressions of confidence.

I want to express my thanks to two pastors who have deeply affected my life. Over the past 11 years, my pastor, Dutch Sheets, has been such an encouragement to me in my walk with Jesus. And Paul Strawn, pastor of North Creek Presbyterian Church in Mill Creek, Washington, greatly encouraged my husband, Jim, and I as I was serving as the U.S. national president of Aglow.

How can I say thanks to Connie Strickland who has been at my side helping me with typing since the beginning of this adventure? Daily for weeks at a time she drove from Denver to Colorado Springs, transcribed tapes and listened to my heart as we colabored together in this process.

And then there is Linda Cagnetti, whom Regal assigned the position of editor. From the beginning, Linda has been a trooper. This book has indeed been a labor of love as Linda, Connie and I all three worked together to birth this baby. I appreciate deeply all the sacrifices they made as well as the encouragement and love they showered on me. This book would never have come to life without Connie's organizational abilities and Linda's great editing skill. Thank you, Connie and Linda, for helping me achieve this goal.

Also my deepest thanks to Carrie Hart, who lives in Israel. What a help she was in editing and giving me writing tips.

I also want to express my thanks to Mary Greenhalge, a prayer partner and a dear friend, who stands with me in the Kingdom purposes of our God here in the Springs.

And, finally, my special heart thanks to my army of Prayer Shield Intercessors who prayed throughout the book-writing process as well as during the heavy travel schedule I maintained. I could never have finished without you.

Foreword

If ever there was a time for prayer, it is the critical hour in which we now find ourselves. If ever there was a time for miracles, it, too, is now! In the uncertainty of the world situation, it is only the power of God that will bring peace to these turbulent times. How do we appropriate that power? On our knees in prayer!

Through this book, you will be encouraged in your prayer life to believe God for miracles that will transform the situations in your personal life as well as being stretched to trust in His power through prayer to impact your community, your region and, ultimately, the nations of the world.

I have known Bobbye Byerly for 20 years as a friend, an intercessor and a leader. She faithfully served in the ministry of Aglow at every level of leadership. Aglow still holds a huge place in her heart, and she continues to be tremendously supportive of all God is doing in the lives of women through this ministry. Bobbye has been a source of encouragement and support to me personally, as she has not only prayed for me but also walked alongside me in her years of service in Aglow.

Bobbye is a woman of prayer, a recognized leader in the prayer movement, and she speaks with strength out of her own life experiences in her journey of prayer with the Lord. You will be inspired from the opening pages as you pursue the Lord's heart in prayer, to be an intercessor, to petition at His throne for miracles. Bobbye's definition of intercession makes it doable for all of us: "Intercession is making yourself available to God, and believing God will hear your prayers."

May you be encouraged by these pages to make yourself available to God!

Jane Hansen
President/CEO
Aglow International

Introduction

My pastor stopped me one day many years ago and said, "Bobbye, God has shown me that He has gifted you with the ministry of intercession. Would you pray for me?"

I looked at him and inquired, "What is intercession?" As he began to explain, I said, "Oh! That is how I enjoy God's presence! I have been an intercessor now for more than 35 years, but I didn't know there was a name for it."

Prayer is the bedrock of my life, and what an adventure it has been and continues to be! Every day brings more passion for intimate communion with God.

I have spent more time in my secret chamber in prayer than in any other place. I *love* meeting with God. The pleasure of His presence is my greatest joy. In fact, the ministry of intercession for me is not so much a burden to pray as it is a burden to love. Love and compassion were Jesus' primary ministry. When He prayed, it was compassion praying that reflected His love and then was released through action. Jesus lived a life of prayer. He is the One after whom I have patterned my life.

In the early 1980s, I heard God refer to me as a weapon of war—His war club; a battle-ax in the hand of God. Scripture confirms this in Isaiah 41:15-16: "Behold, I will make you a new threshing sledge with sharp teeth; you shall thresh the mountains and beat them small, and make the hills like chaff. You shall winnow them, the wind shall carry them away, and the whirlwind shall scatter them; you shall rejoice in the LORD, and glory in the Holy One of Israel." This was my call to intercession, to wage war and bring forth victory in the heavenly realm.

This call isn't only for a select few. We are all called to be women and men of prayer. Why? Because prayer changes everything. It can transform your life and literally change the course of a nation, a city, a church or a family. Think of it! You can actually be involved in reshaping history—even from your home prayer closet. This is the miracle of intercessory prayer and worship.

A dear friend, Dick Eastman, inspired me to more fervent prayer when he wrote about the nations in his book *Love on Its Knees*. According to Eastman, there are some 235 geographical entities we call nations; of these an estimated 97 are all but closed to the gospel or to conventional resident missionary activity. More than 3 billion people live in these "closed" nations.[1] If they are to have access to the gospel, a miracle of intercession must take place. Thanks to an unprecedented global movement of prayer—and multitudes of prayer journeys during the last decade—this miracle has begun to happen.

The promise of the Father to the Son was to send the Holy Spirit. The purpose of the Holy Spirit was and is to reveal Jesus, to bring honor and glory to Him and to fulfill the purposes of the Father on Earth. When we pray in deep intercession, we are cooperating with all three of these purposes. Prayer is bringing forth the passion and unity of the Trinity. I believe Jesus' high-priestly prayer recorded in John 17 is our pattern for prayer, because it is all about the glory of God and unity in the Body of Christ.

We are all called to be intercessors, for intercession is nothing more and nothing less than making yourself available to God and believing He will hear your prayers. If being an intercessor sounds like something beyond your abilities or if you lack faith, please walk with me on my personal journey in prayer and in the power of His presence. Through these pages you will soon see that if God can use an ordinary woman like me to help move His hand, He can use you, too.

There are many wonderful books about prayer and worship. In fact, I have learned from many of them. But my deepest satisfaction comes from years of simply sitting at the feet of Jesus in prayer—this is where we receive the compassionate heart of Christ for all people. By studying His Word, we learn to stand alongside Jesus, the Great Intercessor, to bring about God's plans and holy purposes. He is calling all of us to intimacy with Him, pure and simple. From this place of intimacy, miracles will flow.

Some of the things I have written in this book will not be new to many readers. For others, I hope there may be a new revelation about prayer and worship and about what I mean by the pursuit of holy intimacy. Let us redeem the word "intimacy," which has been so abused in our secular culture today, and reflect on what it means to be invited into deeper intimacy with God.

The stories in this book are His stories. I am His handmaiden, His reporter. I write from the humble perspective of one woman's heart and of a Holy Spirit-led prayer warrior who is still learning new things every day. I consider these pages an adventure story about the miracles wrought in prayer. But more importantly, they tell a love story about one ordinary woman's lifelong pursuit of intimacy with the Lover of her soul. The love of Christ consumes me, and I want all the world to know Him.

Fellow pilgrims, walk with me through this journey in the praying life. The same adventure and romance are available to you if you are available to God. He has no favorites. Each of us is important to Him. You can be assured that He has a unique purpose for you. Ask Him what that purpose is and then listen to what He says.

The stories and lessons in this book come from the trenches of my life experiences and from the continuous teaching and prodding of the Holy Spirit within me. He has led me gently—and sometimes not so gently—into ever higher levels of prayer and intercession and toward deeper and deeper intimacy with Him. I share with you in the hope that what I have written will encourage you in your walk of faith and awaken in you a God-given passion for holy intimacy.

CHAPTER ONE

Living in the Miraculous

I know for sure that miracles happen when we pray. In many years of intercessory praying, I have witnessed many amazing ones, and I believe, too, that the best are yet to come. I'm writing about them to build your faith and your understanding of miracle-producing prayer. But first, I must raise a caution flag about chasing after signs and wonders instead of seeking God, who is the source of them.

I am wary of talking about miracles without *always* calling attention to the Giver of them. The purpose of miracles is to reveal the transforming love and character of God to us, to show us something of what He's like, to woo us to Him. Miracles flow out of holy intimacy with the Holy One—they are the overflow from our personal relationship with Him.

He does not intend miracles to be the exception or a rarity, but rather the norm for His people. Miracles and all supernatural manifestations are the result of His presence in us, in our midst, released in and through us by the Holy Spirit.

When we spend time with Him in prayer and are tutored by the Holy Spirit, we get to know His heart and desires well enough that we become partners with Him. The miracles we are seeing today are simply God's reclaiming the intimacy for which He created us.

Finding Treasures in Broken Vessels

Millions of intercessors around the world today, with upraised hands, are piercing the darkness and propping open the gates of heaven to allow His glory to be revealed throughout the earth. When we fall in love with Him, we become intimate friends with Him, as He always intended. This increases our desire to make Him and His transcendent beautiful love known to others around us. As we pray and worship, this relationship often manifests itself in supernatural ways without our even asking for miracles.

I remember the first time my older son Jim and I worked as counselors with the Billy Graham Crusade. It was at Shea Stadium in New York. The airplanes from La Guardia Airport flew over the stadium, dozens by the hour. On the opening night of training, the Reverend Billy Graham started talking with us from the podium as the engines roared overhead.

He paused, glanced up and quietly said, "We'll have to do something about this noise. This just won't do."

He bowed his head and said a simple prayer to the effect: "Lord, we ask You to shift the wind and send these planes in another direction. Thank You. Amen."

Well, we were believers, but this was a tall order. We weren't sure what, if anything, to expect. But God did it—He answered our prayers in a wondrous way! The morning newspaper reported that the winds had changed during the night and the airplanes over Shea Stadium had to be routed another way. For several days thereafter, thousands of people came to Christ under this anointed leader's preaching. At the conclusion of the crusade, the winds reverted to their normal flow and the airplanes returned to their normal flight patterns.

Well, sure, you say, God listens to Billy Graham, but I'm just an ordinary person.

So am I, precious ones. But I assure you that God wants this kind of simple faith to fill you and flow from you.

Such faith was also evident at the Holy Spirit Celebration in New Orleans in 1988. The German evangelist Reinhardt Bonnke delivered a simple salvation message and closed with a brief invitation, "Any of you who want to accept Christ as your Savior and Lord, please stand up." Some 10,000 people stood up and streamed forward. On the aisle where I was ministering, I saw two men, Dennis and Jeff, whom I knew from the local Lighthouse for the Blind. They recognized my voice and stared into my eyes. "Bobbye, Bobbye, you look wonderful. We can see you," shouted Dennis.

No one had prayed for their healing. No one had touched them, except Jesus, who was there. Quietly, softly He came, wooing and drawing His people to Himself; the healing miracles simply flowed out of His presence. This was a marvelous visitation, but how I yearn for His habitation. There is so much more! Don't you long for the day when we are so saturated with His love and power that when we walk down the street, like the apostle Peter, wherever our shadow falls people are healed?

Another time, I was speaking at a gathering of Aglow Women when a woman came in with a seeing-eye dog. I was fascinated watching the dog lead her. After a time of beautiful worship, I stepped to the microphone and started reading Isaiah 61:

> The Spirit of the Lord God is upon me, because the Lord has anointed Me to bring good news to the suffering and afflicted. He has sent me to comfort the broken-hearted,

> to announce liberty to captives and to open the eyes of the blind (v. 1, *TLB*).

In mid-sentence, I heard the tender, excited voice of a woman seated at a front table.

"George, you're so beautiful," she exclaimed.

She was speaking to her guide dog, George, who had been her eyes for years. Suddenly, she saw him for the first time.

We had not prayed for healing miracles, but they came because God was present in our midst. He was revealing His love and compassion, flowing out of His relationship with many women of prayer gathered in that room.

I saw this happen repeatedly in Argentina, a nation experiencing a decade of tremendous revival. Four times, I have gone to Argentina as an intercessor for the Harvest Evangelism Training Schools and now have been asked by Dr. Peter Wagner to mobilize prayer teams to be prayer shields for the training schools.

During one trip, I was invited to speak at a church in Buenos Aires. The pastor introduced me and advised that I would lead them in a healing service.

"Uh-oh, God," I thought. "I didn't prepare for a healing service. I expected I would only be preaching."

But as I walked toward the podium, I began to feel an overwhelming sense of God's presence in the whole place. The fire of God seemed to burn in my bones. My eyes rested on a woman with a badly scarred face, and in the next instant, her scar disappeared—her skin was transformed like that of a baby. The next moment, I saw three people come out of wheelchairs and start running around the church. I had not come to do a miracle service, but God had. Healings were happening all around me.

So intense was the faith and hunger for God among these people that miracles occurred as a normal part of their prayer and worship.

Reaching the Lost for Christ

The Argentina Revival that started in the early 1980s focused from the beginning on reaching the lost—not on signs and wonders. Many of you have heard of Carlos Annacondia, Claudio and Betty Freidzon, Sergio Scataglini and other leaders in this phenomenal outpouring of God. The miracles flow from their relationship with Christ, because they are devoted completely to God, to His ways, His plans and His purposes. The healing and deliverance miracles, prophecies and other supernatural manifestations build faith among believers, and this draws unbelievers to Jesus. This should not surprise us—remember that sinners have always flocked to Jesus.

This is God's purpose for miracles and supernatural manifestations sweeping the world today. I embrace the words that Pastor Francis Frangipane of River of Life Ministries writes about being wrongly distracted when a spiritual wave or phenomenon sweeps over a church, a city, a country or a personal life.

> It is a spiritual "high tide," where we can be washed and healed. True spiritual waves can release wonderful joy and bring healing to areas within us otherwise untouched by God. Yet, if we are following the waves, we should consider: The tide that comes in with manifestations and blessings also goes out. When the wave is over, it does not mean that God has abandoned us or that His ultimate purpose has changed.
>
> A genuine stirring of God's spirit, either through a fresh doctrinal understanding or through unique spiritual manifestations, is given by God to empower us toward conformity to Christ. Whether we are in a time of preparation or in the glory of a visitation, whether we are

carrying the cross or soaring in resurrection power, our focused, passionate goal must be Christ-likeness.[1]

Remember this about miracles: God does not want us tossed about by the waves but planted in His identity. Prayer is not a device to get God to perform for us; rather, it enables us to

When we walk in holy intimacy with Him, miracles will happen.

absorb His heart as nourishment. Then it's possible to live in a dimension where we experience the continual flow of His grace, peace, love and power. When we walk in holy intimacy with Him, miracles will happen.

And Jesus went about all Galilee, teaching in their synagogues, preaching the gospel of the kingdom, and healing all kinds of sickness and all kinds of disease among the people. Then His fame went throughout all Syria; and they brought to Him all sick people who were afflicted with various diseases and torments, and those who were demon-possessed, epileptics, and paralytics; and He healed them. Great multitudes followed Him—from Galilee, and from Decapolis, Jerusalem, Judea, and beyond the Jordan.

MATTHEW 4:23-25

CHAPTER 2

Laying the Foundation

When I was a little girl, I thought I'd grow up to be a stage star, maybe a ballerina. But God had bigger and better plans for me, so I became an intercessor instead. It's mostly a hidden life, far from the spotlights I imagined as a child. But you sure can't beat it for sheer excitement and fulfillment.

Let me tell you the beginning. I believe that before I came to know God as a real person He was ordering my steps, even though it didn't seem that way when I was young. For many of us, the growing-up years are less than ideal. But through Christ, there is hope and healing for all of us.

I was born in Gilmer, Texas, during the Great Depression. My father drilled rigs for an oil company, so we moved often. My mother suffered from acute clinical depression and was addicted to drugs prescribed to treat her severe headaches. I was separated from her often because she had long stays in mental hospitals, but I did not understand her absences when I was a child.

We grew up living in various communities in Texas, Oklahoma and Illinois, moving with my father's job. Without my mother, he made the best arrangements he could for me and my sister, Jeanne, who was 18 months older than I. Sometimes, Daddy was able to hire help for us; other times, he left us with family members. Thankfully, Jeanne and I did not feel abandoned because we knew Daddy always would come back for us. I remember sitting on a porch in Pearsall, Texas, when we saw Daddy drive up. Jeanne, my feisty sister, turned to me and said, "Here comes that man again. Now we have to leave." We learned early on that when Daddy returned it was usually time for us to move on.

Meeting the Lord in Nana's Faith and Love

As a young girl, I occasionally went to a Methodist church with Daddy, but my background in faith was Catholic. My maternal grandmother was the dominant positive influence in my life. Nana, as we called her, was a strong Irish woman who lived in Henrietta, Oklahoma, a small coal-mining town. Through several hard pinches from her, I learned not to squirm or make noise during Mass. She taught me the fear of the Lord and that church was a place to reverence God; she taught me that God must be first in my life and that He deserved a quiet time of heart preparation as we came into the church to worship.

Jeanne and I spent our summers with Nana, and it was our favorite place to visit. She lived on a farm in a small house with no running water, electricity or indoor bathroom. Though Nana was very poor, we didn't know it. She shared all she had with her neighbors and anyone in need. She raised vegetables, tended multiple fruit trees and two lovely grape arbors. Some of my best memories are of Jeanne and I working alongside her in the garden.

Days with Nana began with attending early morning Mass and receiving Communion. Then, as we walked home from the church, Nana talked about what we were going to have for supper, even though we hadn't even had breakfast yet, as we had fasted until after Communion! With much enthusiasm, Nana planned her entire day around the evening meal. Often she sent Jeanne and me outside to wring a chicken's neck, plunge the bird into water she had heated on a wood stove and pluck its feathers. Almost every evening, she invited people who were poorer than she to have supper with us. Even when there was not much food, this was always a special event that Nana looked forward to.

God has allowed me to draw a parallel between Nana's love for the evening supper and the Marriage Supper of the Lamb. Revelation 19:7-9 says,

> "Let us be glad and rejoice and give Him glory, for the marriage of the Lamb has come, and His wife has made herself ready." And to her it was granted to be arrayed in fine linen, clean and bright, for the fine linen is the righteous acts of the saints. And he said to me, "Write: 'Blessed are those who are called to the marriage supper of the Lamb!'"

Like Jesus wanting to bless His people, Nana desired to bless all those seated around her table. She always left an empty chair at her table for Jesus, since He was the host in her home.

As I see the preparation Mary and Martha always made for Jesus and His disciples, I understand my grandmother's heart for hospitality, as well as my own. Nana's gift of hospitality spilled over into my life and Jeanne's; now we both love when family and friends visit and we enjoy having guests for dinner.

Nana had only four rooms in her home, and all the water we used came from an outdoor well. Not having indoor plumbing, we used an outhouse. And we bathed three times a week in a washtub with water that she heated on her woodstove.

We spent nine summers with Nana and loved every minute. She was a consistent disciplinarian, and after a few spankings, she did not have to say anything more than once to get us to obey. Her strictness, as well as my father's, brought a discipline into my life that has served me well. I now am grateful for their steadfastness in training Jeanne and me that "right is right and wrong is wrong." In a day when godly moral values are scarce, I know absolute truths exist.

Our compassionate Lord healed me and set me free, and He'll do the same for you. He alone has the power to heal our scarred emotions.

I remember a time when I must have been feeling unloved, and I tested Nana's love by throwing her bucket into the well while screaming, "Help, Help!" I then hid under the porch as Nana ran out of the house screaming and sobbing. She shouted into the well, "Bobbye, oh, Bobbye! Are you all right?" Thinking she would be happy to see me, I came out of hiding. At first, she could not believe her eyes. Then she grabbed me and spanked me within an inch of my life, or so I thought. It was painful to sit down for days, but deep in my heart I knew her actions had shown me I was loved. Not having my mother around to love and comfort me, Nana was my excellent substitute.

Sometimes we also lived with my father's dad, who was a widower. He let us get away with many things and usually was kind to us. I remember that he took us once to a drugstore and bought us our first Coca-Cola–what a treat!

But something unusual happened at my grandfather's home when I was five years old. Granddad took me to an outdoor cellar and locked me inside for six hours. Terrified, I cried and hollered for hours, because I didn't know why I was being punished in this way. The experience traumatized me. I never told my father or anyone else what granddad had done, but for years I had nightmares about that dreadful experience. I was 40 years old when Jesus tenderly touched that memory one special day in Scotland and asked me directly, "When are you going to forgive your grandfather?"

I burst into tears. Painful memories surfaced, but I was able, through Jesus' healing love, to release forgiveness to my grandfather.

God will never leave a stone in our hearts unturned. My grandfather had died a few years before, but God knew the painful memory that I harbored because of him. Our compassionate Lord healed me and set me free, and He'll do the same for you. He alone has the power to heal our scarred emotions.

Learning Lessons at the Ranch

Some of our childhood years were spent with aunts living in Oklahoma and Texas. Jeanne and I both enjoyed staying on the ranch in Meridian, Texas, where I developed a love for horses and eventually became a performer in horse shows. Later, in my high school years, Daddy gave me two horses so I could always ride with a friend. Horses and riding were a solace, allowing me to escape the uncertainties of my family life.

Jeanne and I helped our cousin Billy Ray milk the cows, repair fences and tend the sheep. He truly was a gentle shepherd who had only to speak and the sheep followed him. Jeanne and I would try to call the sheep the same way Billy did, but they would not follow us. This experience has helped me to understand more fully the Good Shepherd and how He calls His own by name and we respond to Him.

While living with my father's family in Oklahoma, we attended the Methodist church. Later, Jeanne and I went to the Catholic church and confessed that we had sinned because we had gone to the Methodist church–the priests always understood our confession.

Having a Godly Inheritance

My mother was an only child whose father had abandoned her and Nana when my mother was only a year old. Mother carried that traumatic memory for years. In contrast, my father had a large family–nine sisters and one brother–who all loved and affirmed each other.

In later years, I've come to realize and appreciate the godly inheritance my parents provided. Only now do I see how God's hand was heavy upon me as a child: He was forming something within me that would enable me to embrace His entire Church. As a teenager, I attended youth meetings in both the Catholic and Methodist churches; and although living divided between them was often uncomfortable, I learned much of the love of God in both churches.

At her home in Henrietta, Nana had a threadbare rug next to her bed where she always knelt and prayed. Every morning and evening, Jeanne and I heard her prayers, and, in private, we often made fun of this old-fashioned habit.

But now I thank God for Nana's old-fashioned habit. As I look back, I know Nana's diligent prayers for my entire family had a great impact on our inheritance in the Lord Jesus Christ.

I don't believe we ever fully realize the effectiveness of our prayers. My grandmother's faithful prayers for my mother's healing did not appear to be answered, but there was a time when God revealed Himself to my mother. I believe my grandmother was a vital link to my mother's recovery. Nana, as a mother in her own right, must have suffered heartbreaking pain about her only child's plight, but her devotion to Jesus helped her walk through this painful journey. And she never criticized my father, as she knew he was doing the best he could.

I have other good memories, like when we lived in Durant, Oklahoma, during World War II and Nana moved in to help my father care for us. One of my boyfriends, Skeeter, brought his horse to help my grandmother plow up the backyard for a big garden, and we always had a plentiful harvest, which we shared with our neighbors. All those years living on the farm and ranch taught me the principles of plowing, sowing, weeding and harvesting—the same principles we now see coming to pass in world evangelism.

I also became good friends with some Cherokee children. I rode bikes with them to their homes on the reservation where we hiked the trails, and I learned much about their customs. I discovered that they are very aware of the earth's sounds—and this awareness enhances their sensitivity to the Holy Spirit, a sensitivity I have observed on every prayer journey with Native Americans. It has been my privilege to have deep friendships with many of them, and my heart rejoices in the reconciliation that has taken place with Native Americans over the past decade. They have been set free from past prejudices and judgments to release their gifts into the Body of Christ.

Another Durant, Oklahoma, memory is of a Pentecostal Holiness church, also known as the Holy Rollers church, that we were forbidden to visit. We used to walk there and peek through the windows. And while we were tempted to go inside, we did not want to disobey. It looked and sounded as if the people really liked church—we heard so much joy and laughter coming from inside. Today, I have a deep love for the Pentecostal Holiness church and worship with many friends who are part of that denomination—evidence to me that childhood experiences, good and bad, often have a lasting impact on our adult lives.

My growing years were filled with special memories from every place we lived. My father was a wonderful man who did his best to make our lives happy, and I cannot remember him complaining about his circumstances. He taught us to seize the moment, look for opportunities and make the best of our situation—I still attempt to live by the lessons he taught us.

In the year 2000 at the All Nations Convocation in Israel, I stood worshiping and praising God with people from 205 nations, all praying in their own language. I thought of Golgotha and Jesus' paying the price for all our sins. I reflected on the prayers Nana prayed on that threadbare rug and wondered whether those prayers had traveled with me to six continents. Today I sense that Nana, my mother, father, grandfather, aunts and uncles are peering over the balcony of heaven, delighting in all that is happening in my life.

My frame was not hidden from You, when I was made in secret, and skillfully wrought . . . Your eyes saw my substance, being yet unformed. And in Your book they all were written, the days fashioned for me, when as yet there were none of them.

PSALM 139:15-16

CHAPTER 3

Healing the Past

We had just moved to Houston, Texas, and for the first time, Daddy had bought a home for us. I thought maybe our moving days were over since Daddy was now working in a downtown office.

Experiencing Painful Realities

I was 12 years old and starting new in junior high school, my 17th school to date. I had finally made a few friends and felt like I was leading an almost-normal life. Then, one afternoon as we left school and walked toward home, chattering gleefully about all the things adolescent girls do, reality came crashing back. Along our path, I spotted something ahead of us, on the corner lot near the fence. It looked like a big dog or other large animal lying in the grass, very still.

I felt sick. I had seen this before. "Oh, God," I whispered, "not now, just when I've made new friends."

It was not an animal—it was my mother, drunk or drugged.

Frantic, I deftly chattered to draw attention away from that scene on the other side of the street. Mercifully, it worked. At the corner, I broke off, waited for them to get ahead and then circled back around the block to find my mother.

Two policemen had stopped and were approaching her. She was groaning and thrashing like a caged animal.

"Do you know this woman?" one policeman asked.

"Yes, sir," I replied. "She's my mother. I can take care of her."

I turned to face her. "Get up, Mother. I will take you home," I said softly.

I did not know if it was drugs, alcohol or both this time. The policeman reached to take my mother's arm and she recoiled.

"Let me do it, officer, please," I said frantically. "Just walk behind us at a distance, so she will not make another scene."

This was one of many such episodes of my childhood. Mother suffered severe depression and was emotionally unstable. She had become addicted at an early age to the drugs prescribed for her headaches and was in and out of hospitals for long stretches. Years later, as medical knowledge progressed, she was finally properly diagnosed as suffering from manic depression as well as other emotional problems.

As a child, I barely understood any of this, and my mother's condition seemed to be a taboo topic. Nobody talked about it—except my sister, Jeanne, and I, privately. We shared the secret and were a source of comfort to each other.

I was in the fourth grade in Durant, Oklahoma, when I first realized some truth about my mother. A boy handed me a picture he had drawn of a woman playing cards, smoking a cigarette and holding a bottle in her hand.

"This is your mother," Fred snickered, shoving the drawing in my face.

I was mortified and angry and I defended my mother the only way I knew how: At recess, I marched up to Fred, ripped his shirt, broke his glasses and smashed him with my fists.

I didn't understand exactly why I was so humiliated. I didn't even know my mother very well because she was away in hospitals so often, but I surely didn't see her the way Fred was describing her. My picture may not have been an idealized one, but it was nothing ugly.

There was another scene in the principal's office when Fred's parents arrived. The principal asked why I had acted so violently, but I was too embarrassed to tell the truth, so I took the whipping he gave me. The school contacted my father, and he came to get me: I had been expelled. This was a horror to me, since I had never been expelled and never was again. But that was not the worst that happened to me that day—the worst was hearing my father explain to the principal the truth of why my mother was not living with us now.

The picture Fred drew was closer to reality than mine was. I ached with embarrassment, shame and loneliness.

These days, I cling to some good memories of mother scattered through my teen years. She was stable and home with us for weeks, even months at a time, and when I was 13, she gave birth to a baby boy, whom Jeanne and I named Richard Wayne Carter. He was a joy and delight to our family. His arrival allowed us to enjoy a normal family life. Then a dark cloud appeared; mother's depression returned, and she left again for treatment.

For years, I carried guilt that somehow I was responsible for my mother's illnesses. As a small child, I accidentally overheard a great aunt say about my mother: "There would be nothing wrong with Margaret if it were not for those two little girls."

Those words pierced my heart and stuck like a thorn that only became more firmly embedded over the years, and I carried this guilt for more than 20 years. Unintentionally, my great aunt's words had spoken death instead of life to me. They put me in a bondage that God never intended—bondage that kept me from experiencing the expression of freedom I was meant to have in Christ Jesus. This bondage promotes sin, holding Christians captive to things that hinder the abundant and effective Spirit-filled life God has planned for them. Years later, God would free me through a better understanding of His Word and through His supernatural power.

HEALING HIDDEN WOUNDS

I've been privileged and blessed to minister to women across America and around the world. I have seen the devastating effects of unhealed childhood wounds, many of which are directly related to alcoholic parents, drug abuse, rage, neglect, abandonment, verbal and physical abuse, incest and more. We stuff our feelings away deep inside and disguise the weight of our insecurity, inadequacy and sadness with a bright smile and surface poise. We silently grieve for what never was; we suffer

I have learned to see myself as He sees me, as "His beloved."

from anger and shame. Fear of rejection and abandonment causes many disorders. We try to overcontrol our lives because we do not have the capacity to trust, and we cover the truth and live disillusioned lives.

Damaged emotions affect all our relationships—unless they are healed by the love of God. Coping is not the same as healing. I did not know true freedom until Jesus Himself set me free.

God has touched my personal life with incredible miracles, and He has allowed me to participate in and witness miracles around the world. But there is no more transforming healing than our own inner healing. God healed hurts in my heart that no one else could reach or knew about—He plucked out the intractable thorns.

This miracle was not instantaneous, and I have had to be patient and grow through His healing process. I have learned to see myself as He sees me, as "His beloved." I have learned to redefine myself by who I am *in Him*.

We all need His healing touch. If He did it for me, He will do it for you. Ask Him. His abundant, tender love will soothe your hurts, and He will restore and empower you to become all He desires you to be. You will experience wholeness you never thought possible.

Embracing the God of Resurrection Life

My mother struggled with mental illness and life-robbing addictions for 27 years before God delivered her. I do not know why He allows certain things in our lives, but I know that God promises to bring good out of troubles we must encounter, so long as we love Him, and if we allow and trust Him to use them for His purposes (see Rom. 8:28).

When we seek Him for deliverance, we come to know the Deliverer. When we ask for healing, we meet the Healer. We come to know our Savior in deeper dimensions, and knowing Him brings us closer to being conformed to His image. He gave up His former glory and honor to come to Earth and die on a cross that we might be restored to a life of fellowship with the Father and live this life abundantly. He is the God of resurrection life. I am mindful of this miracle every day.

All of us have good and bad in our past, but God helps us to keep and treasure the good and bury the rest in Him. He came to set the captives free, but we must be willing to let Him do it. Then, we can walk as healers in a world riddled with sin, pain, disillusionment, discouragement and lack of faith. He wants us to be vessels He can use to release His presence and miracles into this world. But before He can use those vessels, He wants to purify them—by rooting out and healing old wounds and scars. We can no longer be victims; today He's calling forth spiritual warriors to be victors who can minister filled with His love and His power.

God Remembers Our Prayers

I prayed for Mother for years and it seemed my prayers would never be answered. Once I cried out to the Lord that Mother's life was wasted, and I was stunned when I sensed God say to me, "What I have given breath to, don't call wasted."

One day many years later, while we were visiting, Mother startled me with a question: "Bobbye, how did you continue to love me despite the drugs and drinking?"

God remembered all my prayers.

I was honored to share with my mother about my Savior, Jesus Christ. Our tears flowed together.

"Do you think Jesus would accept me now that I am 55 and never really knew Him?" she asked.

What a glorious moment! He delivered my mother from 27 years of bondage and torment.

Mother became a visionsharer with older people living in the local nursing home. She told them how Christ had come into her life after years of darkness and always ended her conversations with the invitation, "Would you like to accept Him?"

God not only saved Mother, He also turned her into a caring person.

A year later, in 1967, we moved back to New Jersey, and Mother was coming to live with us. The night she arrived, she was excited about my brother Richard's upcoming wedding. She told us all about Richard's fiancée, Helen, whom we had not met. We caught her up on news of my sister, Jeanne, her husband, Bill, and their children, who were all coming to dinner the following night. All evening, Mother talked and laughed with us—she was so pleased about the settled nature of her three children's lives.

The next morning, when I went to wake her, I found she had died in her sleep. The initial shock was tremendous, but my comfort was that I knew she had gone to be with the Lord.

When I think of her now, I know that from the balcony of heaven she is one of my greatest cheerleaders.

I waited patiently for the LORD; and He inclined to me, and heard my cry. He also brought me up out of a horrible pit, out of the miry clay, and set my feet upon a rock, and established my steps. He has put a new song in my mouth—praise to our God; many will see it and fear, and will trust in the LORD.

PSALM 40:1-3

CHAPTER 4

Encounter with Jesus

There's no pretty way to say it. I was 28 years old and miserable. I had moved four times in 10 years of marriage, and the last time we moved, I had left both my parents in Houston hospitals, and my 15-year-old brother had gone to live with an aunt and uncle. Then my father, whom I adored, died. He had been my hero, and now I was flying from my home in New Jersey to Texas for his funeral.

Looking back at that time, it was obvious that my marriage was falling apart. My husband, Jim, who traveled extensively, seemed married to his job. We had three small sons, the youngest only two years old, and I'd lost two babies in miscarriages, which probably added to the strain in our marriage.

My semi-invalid mother-in-law, Maggie, had lived with us for nine years and required considerable care. As a result, I blamed her for almost everything wrong in my life.

My family went to church faithfully, and I desired to be a good wife and mother; but I had lost the capacity to love. I had many friends, and, at one time, a deep, loving relationship with my husband. Yet, now, the power to love and to overcome the stress in my life was gone, and I felt as if I were living with a bag covering my head and I could not breathe.

But on the way to that funeral, God had a divine appointment for me.

Do You Know My Jesus?

My husband was away at job training, so I was flying alone. I was startled when a Japanese man seated next to me said politely, "Lady, you seem troubled."

I brushed his concern aside, but he persisted.

Suddenly my tears came, and I told him my father had just died.

"Do you know Jesus Christ?" he asked.

What a question to ask *me!* I was an American woman who had always gone to church.

He patiently repeated his query. "Do you know my Jesus?"

I didn't answer him, but turned away and stared silently out the window, contemplating the turn of events in my life.

Soon I would see my mother, who had just been released from a mental hospital. My sister and brother would be at the funeral as well as many of the aunts and uncles who had helped my dad rear us during my mom's numerous hospitalizations.

Within a few hours my plane arrived in Houston. I made it through the funeral and spent time visiting my relatives, but the Japanese traveler's question haunted me.

I kept wondering, *Did I know Jesus? I thought I did, but what did the traveler really mean?*

My doubts drove me to seek counsel from my pastor. Earlier we had agreed to meet for six sessions starting in mid-April. I had told him about my plan for the boys and me to leave Jim and his mother, so he knew I was serious about a June 10 departure date. I would be 30 years old and surely I could make a better life for myself and the boys somewhere else.

On June 8, I entered the pastor's office for my last counseling session. He had attempted to reveal truth to me during our previous meetings, but I was living in darkness, unable to receive light. It was as if I were deaf to every suggestion he made and blind to my own insecurities. I had continually told him that I was fine and that it was just Jim's mother I could not live with. I did love my husband, I confessed, but enough was enough. Meanwhile, I had not told Jim's mother I was leaving. When my pastor questioned me on this point, I said, "Jim can handle that."

Then, without thinking about it, I blurted out, "A man seated next to me on the plane as I was flying to Daddy's funeral asked me if I knew Jesus. The question is haunting me. Do you think I know Jesus?"

My pastor must have been shocked. I was a Sunday School teacher and president of the women's group at our church. Jim and I were both active in our congregation, as were our children, and on the surface, my life looked good. But I knew I was like the "whitewashed tombs" Jesus described in Matthew 23:27–beautiful on the outside, but inside full of dead men's bones and all uncleanness.

I can't fully explain what happened in the next few moments after my question about Jesus. The light of God's glory supernaturally filled the pastor's office, and I then fell on my face before a holy God, weeping profusely. The light in the room was so intensely bright that I could not look at it. I suddenly saw myself a sinner in need of a Savior. I found myself confessing my sins–everything I had denied during the past six weeks. Jesus was taking away all my filth, but He was not condemning me or judging me. He was simply and miraculously setting me free of the fear and bitterness that was swallowing me, while waves of God's love and grace washed over me repeatedly.

I was a broken, confused, sinful woman who was encountering the living Lord Jesus. I had read the Bible from Genesis to

Revelation for two consecutive years, and while I loved the stories, the words were just words to me. Suddenly, by the quickening power of the Holy Spirit, that changed, and the written word of God became living and active in me. He was personalizing His Word just for me. I picked up my pastor's Bible and it opened to Deuteronomy 30:19-20:

> I call heaven and earth as witnesses today against you, that I have set before you life and death, blessing and cursing; therefore choose life, that both you and your descendants may live; that you may love the LORD your God, that you may obey His voice, and that you may cling to Him, for He is your life and the length of your days; and that you may dwell in the land which the LORD swore to your fathers, to Abraham, Isaac, and Jacob, to give them.

I stood up and declared boldly to God, "I choose life! I choose life for me, and my descendants–my sons, Jim, John and Bob!" (I confess, at the time, I could not choose life for Jim or his mother.)

This was the second time God had turned me from death to life. The first time was during my senior year in high school, when my father spoke words of life into my paralyzed body, even as doctors gave him little hope that I would ever recover from spinal meningitis. Three weeks later, I was fully healed and walked out of the hospital. I was able to attend my prom and graduation.

Now, in the pastor's office, still weeping, I opened his Bible again, this time to Ezekiel 36:25-27. I sensed God was speaking directly to me–I had never felt that way before.

> Then I will sprinkle clean water on you, and you shall be clean; I will cleanse you from all your filthiness and from

all your idols. I will give you a new heart and put a new spirit within you; I will take the heart of stone out of your flesh and give you a heart of flesh. I will put My Spirit within you and cause you to walk in My statutes, and you will keep My judgments and do them.

I chose life, and now God was giving me the power of the Holy Spirit to live in Him. What an overwhelming revelation! Only the Holy Spirit can reveal Jesus' transforming love for us and make God real and personal to us. What a miracle! I was a changed woman but did not fully realize it. Whenever I tell this story, I share that, on that special day, I felt like a worm as I entered the pastor's office, but came away feeling like a chirping canary!

Only the Holy Spirit can reveal Jesus' transforming love for us and make God real and personal to us.

I lost track of the time in that room, not realizing I had been in there for six hours! I rushed to get home because I had never before left my mother-in-law unattended for that long.

All I could think about was that something miraculous had happened to me. The gray world along the highway was now in technicolor, and the trees bulged with lush green leaves and the flowers burst with blooms. I had been in such darkness that I had not seen spring arrive. Like the biblical woman at the well, I had an unexpected date with destiny; like her, I had personally met Jesus, and I wanted to run and tell somebody. So, I raced into my house and up the stairs to Maggie's room. I sat on her bed, put my arms around her and said, "Mom, I love you."

"I know you do, honey," she replied matter-of-factly.

"No, Mom, I *really* love you," I said, staring intently into her clear, blue eyes. Then I told her what had happened to me in the pastor's office.

In the next instant, His miraculous love healed us both—her of a cardiovascular infirmity which had made her semi-invalid for nine years, and me of debilitating resentment and bitterness.

My marriage began afresh, too. That evening, I told Jim I wanted to stay and make our marriage work. He was delighted, admitting that he had never wanted me to leave him. I fell in love again with the special guy I had married, and his mother actually became my closest friend. My sons rejoiced that our family would not be broken. Isn't God amazing?

Maggie and I became prayer partners, praying regularly for the entire family. I no longer nagged God to change Jim, because I was content in the love of Jesus.

Will You Stand in the Gap?

One year later, the night after his high school graduation party, my brother, Richard, tried to beat an oncoming train by veering around a barricade. The speeding train hit Richard's car broadside, breaking two bones in his neck, crushing his skull, severing the optic nerve in his right eye and breaking 40 other bones in his body. He was pronounced dead at the hospital, and I received a phone call telling me the tragic news.

I was living in New Jersey at the time, and it took me 10 hours to get to Houston. During the flight, I cried out to Jesus for His mercy. Little did I know that I was in for another shock.

After pronouncing my brother dead, the doctors had done exploratory surgery to learn more about severe trauma. During the surgery, they discovered that Richard was alive but in a coma. The doctors gave him a 10 percent chance to live.

I stayed with Richard each night. On the fourth night, as I dozed and prayed, a man I'd never seen before came into the room, praising the Lord loudly.

"Shhh, there is someone here who is very sick," I said.

"Oh, I know, sister. I'm the ambulance driver who picked this young fool up at the railroad track. I asked God to raise him from the dead so he would not dwell in hell for eternity but would have an opportunity to come to know Jesus Christ and live eternally with God."

I stared at him dumbfounded. Here I was, a new Christian who believed in God and knew Jesus as my personal Savior. I'd seen my mother-in-law healed and my marriage restored. My walk with God was intact. But, I had never met anyone who had the boldness and confidence in God that this man had.

He stood by Richard's bed and proclaimed: "Live! I command this body to live. I command all these bones to be healed. I command this brain to mend and there be no brain damage. Lord, from the top of his head to the soles of his feet, heal this young man. Allow him to walk and talk again. You will live, Richard, and you will be totally healed and walk out of this hospital. Yes, you will! Yes, you will!"

Miraculously, Richard came out of the coma. During his long recovery, many friends visited to encourage him. He fully recovered, had suffered no brain damage, and the optic nerve in his right eye repaired itself. Glory be to our God!

From that day to this, I have thanked God for a praying ambulance driver who was full of the Lord. I had never seen anything like that man's faith. After I received the Holy Spirit in a new way in my life, I knew that I had seen and experienced the Holy Spirit's supernatural power through the ambulance driver. He was an intercessor who stood in the gap for people in crisis, willingly becoming a bridge between the kingdom of light and the kingdom of darkness.

With intercessory prayer, people like that ambulance driver reach up for God with one hand and down to men, women and children with the other. They hold them before the throne of God alongside Jesus, the great Intercessor.

It took a few years for my brother, Richard, to come to know God. He used to brag that he was indestructible, and although I knew the real story of what had happened in that hospital, I was unable to relate it to him for years. God met my brother at another point of need and called Richard to Himself. The great Intercessor, Jesus, was there all the time, pleading on Richard's behalf.

I also learned the benefit of persistent, persevering prayer as I prayed fervently for Richard, his wife, Helen, and their two sons to come to know Jesus Christ as Lord and Savior. That prayer has also been answered.

Centuries ago George Whitefield wrote: "The renewal of our natures is a work of great importance. It is not to be done in a day. We have not only a new house to build up, but an old one to pull down."[1]

"Do not let your hearts be troubled. Trust in God; trust also in me. In my Father's house are many rooms; if it were not so, I would have told you. I am going there to prepare a place for you. And if I go and prepare a place for you, I will come back and take you to be with me that you also may be where I am. You know the way to the place where I am going." Thomas said to him, "Lord, we don't know where you are going, so how can we know the way?" Jesus answered, "I am the way and the truth and the life. No one comes to the Father except through me."

JOHN 14:1-6 (*NIV*)

CHAPTER 5

Deep Water

After you read the New Testament book of Acts, it's hard to settle for ordinary, ho-hum Christianity. Why shouldn't today's followers of Jesus experience the same supernatural power, love and joy that the first Christians did? Knowing that God is real, why shouldn't we live freely in the same gifts and fruit of the Holy Spirit as those Pentecost believers?

MEET THE HOLY SPIRIT

I was soon to learn the answers to these questions. In 1967, I was teaching a Bible study on the book of Acts—and I had managed to cover the first 18 chapters without personally meeting the Holy Spirit. My hunger, however, was growing for God to bring these New Testament gifts, with their ensuing miracles, to my church.

That night, in the middle of my teaching, I sensed something different stirring in my spirit. When I opened my mouth, I was surprised at what I said. I began to tell the whole class that God wanted to empower us and our church through the gifts of the Holy Spirit right now.

My pastor interrupted me. "I am concerned that you are getting into deep water, Bobbye. You are getting into something emotional," he said. "Your mother, who just died, was emotionally disturbed, and I am now concerned for you. I have known others to get off track on these things."

He asked if I had ever spoken in tongues.

"No," I said, "but I know I will." My words shocked me, since I had no previous desire to speak in tongues, nor did I know anyone who did.

My pastor stopped the meeting and advised my husband, Jim, to get me under control. "Bobbye has gotten into deep water and will drown," he warned.

I was surprised at his words and at the same time bewildered by the unexplainable joy bubbling inside my spirit. "Bobbye won't be teaching anymore," he told the group. "Next week, we'll meet at my house." As these friends left, they said they loved the teaching but did not understand it.

I somehow knew I was experiencing a touch from the Holy Spirit. I was truly being filled with unspeakable joy as His presence seemed to surround me.

"I don't understand either," I admitted, "but I know the Lord wants to do something special in our midst."

I could not sleep that night, wondering what was happening to me. I knew little about Holy Spirit baptism or infilling except what I'd read in Acts. And tongues? I recalled having received a letter several years ago from a previous pastor, Brick Bradford, who wrote that he had been "baptized in the Holy Spirit with evidence of speaking in tongues." As a result, the Presbytery had asked him to relinquish his pastorate. I had not replied to the letter because I did not understand what he was saying. Lying on my bed, now, I somehow knew I was experiencing a touch from the Holy Spirit.

Suddenly I sat upright. Unrecognizable words, not English ones, were flowing spontaneously out of my mouth.

I hopped out of bed and hurried to the living room. I sat in the dark, and the "tongues" came again. I was babbling, laughing, crying and truly being filled with unspeakable joy as His presence seemed to surround me. The darkness became light to me, and I gloriously praised the Lord in a new way.

Once during the night, my oldest son came into the hall and asked, "Mom, what are you doing?"

I stopped to answer him. "I am in the presence of the Lord, son, and I do not know what is happening." It seemed that he was standing in the darkness and that light enveloped me. That was my first understanding of spiritual warfare. I wanted my son to come into the light, so I asked him to come near me, but he warily refused. As he started back to bed he said, "Mom, could you be a little quieter?"

I prayed all night, asking God for an explanation of what was happening to me, but I got no answer. The next day, I searched the Scriptures, but I still was unsure how to interpret my strange experience.

"You Will Not Drown"

Two days later, there was a knock at my door. A young mother I had never seen before was standing in the doorway holding two babies. "I have never done this before," she said nervously.

"What are you going to do?" I asked.

I did not know what she was going to do, but I invited her inside nonetheless. She said the Lord had guided her to my home from a neighboring community. "I have a word from the Lord for you," she said. "He told me to tell you this: 'You must come to Me walking on the water, with no sure accustomed earth beneath your feet, for the One to whom you come is the Son of God and the Son of Man.'" She paused, puzzled, then added, "He also says, you will not drown!"

I remembered those words 15 years in August of 1982 when sailing in the Gulf of Mexico with dear family friends. Our son, Bob, who was on summer break from college, and I met them in Destin, Florida. Although Bob had given his heart to Jesus at age 10, was gloriously baptized in the Holy Spirit at 12 and had been a youth leader who was much loved by the children he ministered to, Bob was now rebelling against God. How my heart grieved for this son of mine!

While attending a Christian college, "scholars" taught him that the gifts of the Spirit are no longer applicable in the Church today. This had caused Bob much confusion, which ultimately led him down a path of spiritual rebellion, and was the occasion for much fervent prayer on his behalf. At times, while driving down the street, I had to pull over to the side of the road as I wept in intense intercession for him. But I had seen no change in Bob.

Our youngest son, Bob, holds a special place in my heart because his birth was truly a gift from God. Before he was born, I had suffered two miscarriages and was told I would never have another child.

On the beach in Destin, Bob asked me to go sailing. I loved him so deeply. My intense desire to have our relationship healed prompted me to say yes, even though I did not know how to swim and I had a serious fear of water.

We were quite far out on the Gulf when a fierce windstorm suddenly developed. The next thing I knew, our catamaran flipped over, and I was spiraling down, down and could not stop.

Then, suddenly, the downward motion reversed, and I felt myself being propelled upward. I surfaced, gasped for air and began to kick my feet and splash with my hands. This seemed to keep my head above the cold waves that were lapping mercilessly over me. One of my friends, Paul, standing on the upended hull, frantically motioned me to swim toward him. When I did not respond to his motions, he shouted over the wind, "Bobbye, swim to shore!"

It was too late to tell him I did not know how to swim.

I watched hopelessly as the tide pushed the overturned catamaran farther and farther away from me, while my friends were clinging onto it.

Knowing I would soon drown, I asked God, "Am I confessed up-to-date? Is there any sin separating me from You?" I expected to see Jesus momentarily. My destiny was written, finished, but inexplicably, the peace of God enveloped me. I began to pray in tongues and to quote Scripture as I waited to die. Remarkably, I had no fear. I asked God only one thing, "Lord, when Jim, my family and friends learn that I have drowned, let them have the same peace I am experiencing at this moment."

I believe that the years of prayer and delight in the throne room of God were my strength in the tumultuous sea.

After a time, I saw three young men paddling furiously on surfboards. My first thought was they should not be out here because the water was so rough. As they paddled closer, it suddenly dawned on me they were coming to my rescue. My prayers changed in an instant. "God, help them hurry!"

When they finally arrived, one of the rescuers pushed me onto his surfboard. He said his friends had already called the Coast Guard and reported a casualty, but to his amazement, I was not in shock and wouldn't even need their oxygen. On our way back to the shore, we stopped for a brief rest on a sandbar.

Then I recognized Bob swimming furiously toward us.

"You have a very brave mother," the lifeguard told Bob.

"No," Bob responded, "she has a mighty God! She does not even know how to swim."

The lifeguard was aghast. "How did you stay up in the water for 40 minutes?" he asked. "Most swimmers can only swim for seven minutes when caught in a riptide." I learned that a riptide occurs when opposing currents clash, causing violent disturbance in the water. Amazed that I had stayed afloat on the violent water all that time, I replied, "The Lord held me up."

"You are very lucky," the lifeguard said. "My buddy climbed on the lifeguard stand and thought he saw someone bobbing in the water. We thought it was impossible for anyone to survive in that water, but the three of us decided to go out together to check it anyway." My friends made it to shore hanging onto the overturned catamaran.

My son and I hugged each other, joyfully sharing in the knowledge that a miracle had just happened. He fell to his knees on the sandy beach and began to weep. The Holy Spirit tugged at his heart, and he now knew he could trust the Lord. Today, all these years later, he and his precious family faithfully serve Him.

The words spoken to me by my pastor 15 years earlier–that I was getting into deep water and would drown–had not come to pass. The Word of God stored in my heart and the gift of tongues were my lifeline in the raging sea.

I thank God for the day that young mother came to my door with the assuring words from the Lord, "You will not drown." I am grateful that the "emotional experience" was in reality an empowering of the Holy Spirit.

God is the God of faithfulness and miracles. That day on the beach was a two-miracle day for my family: God saved me from physical death and restored my son to spiritual life.

Fear not, for I have redeemed you; I have called you by your name; you are Mine. When you pass through the waters, I will be with you; and through the rivers, they shall not overflow you. When you walk through the fire, you shall not be burned, nor shall the flame scorch you. For I am the LORD your God, the Holy One of Israel, your Savior.

ISAIAH 43:2

CHAPTER 6

Love and Laughter

I was never one to be satisfied with just one thing—I wanted fullness of life. God blessed me with passion for everything from ballet to baseball games with my father. I went to church regularly and often to multiple churches, so the Lord revealed Himself to me in different ways and through various styles of worship.

I sense that God knew when I met Jesus personally and was baptized by the Holy Spirit that I wanted a life-changing encounter, not a gentle, average makeover.

Thirty-five years later when I read Tommy Tenney's book about God Chasers, I cheered, "Yes, count me in!" That's what I had been doing long before Tommy gave us a name for it.

God will use ordinary women and men for extraordinary things if we seek fellowship and intimacy with Him.

"There is so much more of God available than we have ever known or imagined," Tommy writes in *The God Chasers*. "But we have become so satisfied with where we are and what we have that we don't press in for God's best."[1]

We know all *about* God; we do good things in His name. We ache for a life-transforming encounter like

Paul on the Damascus Road, but we settle for less than the best He has for us. We stop way short of seeking *intimacy* with Him—which is what He wants most of all. Our prayers are powerless because our passion to know Him is weak.

But God's Word says, "Blessed are those who hunger and thirst for righteousness, for they shall be filled" (Matt. 5:6). If we pray out of hunger and thirst for Him, I promise you He *will* show up—in awesome, life-changing, sovereign ways. My whole life is proof of this.

Miracle Praying 101

Shortly after I received the baptism in the Holy Spirit in 1967, five of my friends came to my house weekly for a prayer meeting. Within a few months, we had 60 to 100 women coming from churches all over Bergen County, New Jersey. We called ourselves the Love and Laughter prayer group because we loved God with all our hearts and laughed with joy at the wonderful things He did in our midst.

We were novices to the workings of the Holy Spirit, but the Holy Spirit didn't seem to mind. He always showed up. As my mentor and fellow intercessor friend, Joy Dawson, says, we were "spoiled for the ordinary," as God was teaching us about His character, and that miracles were His norm, not the exception.

One woman always brought her friend Linda, who was suffering from chronic depression. But instead of attending our prayer meetings, Linda slept upstairs in my son's bed during the entire prayer time.

Nonetheless, my friend, who was absolutely sold out to God, brought Linda faithfully and routinely put her to bed after they arrived. While she slept, we were in the basement family room praying for her and others.

One day, Linda appeared on the stairs. "I want to be a part of this group. I want to be prayed for," she announced. "I want to be healed of my depression." Then she declared without our asking, "I want to accept Christ."

We prayed; she met Jesus as Savior, and at that moment she was set free from her debilitating depression. She was a different woman, coming weekly to pray instead of hiding and sleeping. To this day, as far as I know, Linda still is ministering to others and sharing the love of Jesus.

Another member of our group, who was with us for two years, brought a friend of hers, Cutchie, an 80-year-old woman who was blind. Unexpectedly, during one prayer meeting, Cutchie turned to me and said, "You are Bobbye. I can see you. You are beautiful."

I smiled at her. "Cutchie, have your blind eyes been opened?" I asked.

Looking around the room, she started identifying each woman by name as they spoke. Then she spotted our youngest member Georgia, who was walking toward her. Cutchie said, "You wear your skirts too short, Georgia." Miniskirts were stylish in those days. We laughed. We loved to watch the way God worked.

Wherever the Holy Spirit shows up, people are drawn there. Word of our homegrown prayer meetings spread.

One Wednesday, I answered my ringing doorbell to find a Catholic priest on my porch. "I hear that several of my parishioners attend your weekly prayer meetings," he said. "I have come to check them out."

I invited him in and explained that I did not know which churches were represented since our focus was simply Jesus. As we began to pray, the Holy Spirit was already moving, and Father Jim Ferry joined in with enthusiasm. At one point some were praying deliverance over a woman when Father Jim began to laugh. Thinking this a little strange, I walked over to see what was happening. He explained, "I was just reading about Lydia, the seller of purple, when I heard the Holy Spirit telling me to come to your house. Here you are, Bobbye, dressed in a purple linen dress. I have just received my confirmation that God wants me to be part of this." All of us rejoiced. He was our only man, but others would follow.

Father Ferry was baptized in the Holy Spirit in 1967 at the University of Duquesne Outpouring. We established a deep friendship and laughed for years that we cut our teeth together in the Holy Spirit.

Another day, a friend from New York State phoned my New Jersey home and told me her neighbor's grandchild had been born deformed. "Bobbye, I have heard strange, wonderful stories about you and your prayer group," she said. "Could I bring Sue and her grandson to your house for prayer?"

I gathered seven of Love and Laughter's strongest intercessors the day Sue and her grandson came. The baby was severely deformed, and the parents were told they had to wait several years before surgeons could attempt to align his hips and shoulders and that several surgeries would be required.

We talked and prayed at length with the baby's mother, Eleanor, and grandmother, Sue. They both accepted Christ that day.

"This is why God really brought them here," I thought. I served lunch and we talked. But I then realized we were not finished with our prayers when Eleanor said, "Bobbye, you have not yet prayed for my baby."

I picked up Jason, his face pallid, his little body drawn. I held him in my arms, thinking, *O God, please lead us*. We all gathered around, prayed a gentle prayer and anointed him with oil.

"Look! Look at his complexion," Eleanor said excitedly. "He has color." His tiny cheeks had begun to glow, but in our inexperience, we did not recognize this as a healing sign.

Two weeks later, Eleanor called. "Jason's family took him to Presbyterian Children's Hospital in New York for his checkup. The doctor reported to them that the baby's hips and shoulders were properly aligned.

Grandmother Sue became a full-fledged member of Love and Laughter, driving more than an hour every Wednesday to attend.

When God Doesn't Answer as We Want

During this Love-and-Laughter era, God also taught me a lesson about trusting Him when things don't work out as we think they should.

When my friend Helen learned she had cancer, I drove to her house, which was some distance from me, to pray for her. I told her about the weekly prayer meeting at my home and some of the miracles we had experienced.

"I would love to come," Helen said, "but I don't know much about Jesus." I made arrangements with a friend to bring Helen every Wednesday. Soon, she accepted Christ—the greatest miracle—and we prayed fervently for her healing. Her faith grew by leaps and bounds.

Then in 1970, Shell Oil Company unexpectedly moved its headquarters to Houston, Texas. This meant once again uprooting and moving our family and other Shell family friends.

We moved to Houston in hot July, and within a few days of settling into a new house, two neighbors, Mary Beth Wurts and Shirley Caulton, came by to welcome us. They had heard from another friend about the New Jersey Love and Laughter group and asked if I would start a prayer meeting in my Houston home.

"Let's ask God what *He* thinks about it," I said. So we sat amid my unpacked boxes and prayed. I did not want to do something, presuming that God would bless it, so I've learned to ask Him first. I believed He said yes, so we started a Wednesday prayer meeting. Many of the original Love and Laughter members, who'd also moved to Houston joined the newcomers.

Helen was one of the Houston transplants. Despite our prayers, she never received the fullness of her healing. As her cancer progressed, we continued to love her and hold her before God's throne in intercessory prayer.

The enemy hates persistent, fervent prayer, and I was about to learn this lesson big-time.

As we prayed for Helen, persecution arose against me, and I was accused of giving Helen false hope about her healing.

"You have deceived Helen by making her think she was going to be healed," one woman scolded me.

Helen loved all of us and came to our prayer meetings until she was physically unable. She then asked several of us to come to her home and pray with her, so we did—until her husband forbade it.

I knew Helen was suffering much pain, and it broke my heart when her daughter phoned and pleaded with me to visit her mother.

"I cannot come to the house," I said, without explaining that her father had forbidden it, "but be assured I will pray at home."

When Helen died, it took all the courage I could muster to attend her funeral. When her daughter saw me, we fell into each other's arms weeping. "Just before Mom died, she told me why you couldn't come and pray with her," the daughter sobbed. "Please forgive my father."

"I forgave him long ago," I assured her.

But my heart was heavy, and my faith was severely tested. "I don't know if I can continue, Father," I prayed, grieving. "This has been the most painful experience I have known."

A few days after the funeral, I heard God ask me in my spirit, "Will you now step over the pain and trauma you've experienced with Helen and go on to the next assignment I have for you?"

I was at a loss for answers. I had been severely judged and did not want to misguide His precious children. I was very frank with God, and I poured out my heart to Him, having faith that He knows all our questions and that He alone is the answer.

As our experiences and friendship with God grow, we slowly develop a deep trust that is the doorway that leads to intimacy with Him.

When the next prayer assignment came, God graced me to overcome my doubts and fears. Faith rose up within me. I had prayed for many people who were desperately ill and saw God miraculously touch them. Others, I had simply released to His greater plan. As our experiences and friendship with God grow, we slowly develop a deep trust that is the doorway leading to intimacy with Him.

Meanwhile, I hung on to Psalm 16:11: "You will show me the path of life; in Your presence is fullness of joy; at Your right hand are pleasures forevermore."

Whenever we have a fresh revelation of the deep love of Christ, we are overwhelmed. At the time of my deepest searching before the Lord, I confessed to the lover of my soul, "Your love, O Christ, exceeds all the joys and sorrows of this world. You have erased my doubts and fears and any concern that I had for my reputation. You are my God, and I will trust you."

I had lost Helen as well as several close friends who had turned against me, and others who were disappointed with me. But I was deeply touched by what Amy Carmichael writes: "There are times when spiritual discernment is the chief gift of the Spirit. The praised and made-much-of seldom have it. But those who have suffered the loss of all things, even their reputation—these if they live with their Lord, have this gift."[2]

I believe the enemy sows tares of doubt along with the good seed of the miracle one has experienced. This can cause some people to lose their miracle of healing. The miracle of intercessory prayer is that we love God's people and hold them before His throne whether or not we see results, knowing that God has a divine purpose for each of our lives.

I encourage you, don't give up praying even when it appears hopeless. God's ways are not our ways. I've been bewildered and awestruck at the wondrous, creative ways He draws the lost to Him and heals through prayers we thought He never heard. He hears and remembers, and I love His creativity.

Let me tell you about Jane, a friend who had multiple sclerosis. She was filled with bitterness and anxiety. Taking turns with other church friends, I drove Jane to therapy once a week for a year, but her illness only got progressively worse.

One day, her husband, Richard, called and asked me if I really believed in divine healing. He said his son had come home from Sunday School and told him, "Mrs. Byerly really believes what she teaches."

At Richard's request, we met several times to go through the Bible looking up verses about healing. Richard wrote all of them down in longhand and filled five pages, front and back, with healing verses he planned to pray over his wife.

Soon after this, when our family moved to Houston, I heard from friends that Richard had suffered a massive heart attack and died instantly. Jane was left alone, not only physically broken, but heartbroken, too. She grew weaker and was confined to a wheelchair. Then her two boys departed from God's ways, causing Jane more grief.

But one day I received a startling phone call from Jane. She had wheeled herself into her husband's office, and at that moment his Bible fell to the floor. Her nurse came running, saw the scattered papers, scooped them up and handed them to Jane. This was Richard's Bible, stuffed with papers on which he had written "Healing prayers for Jane, by Dick and Bobbye." His heart had been focused on his wife's healing, the same as my heart had been. From His Word, we had both been praying what was on God's heart for Jane.

When Jane began reading the healing verses aloud, God heard and visited her. "Bobbye," she said, "God miraculously healed me. I am no longer in a wheelchair. The pain, bitterness and anger I felt after Richard's death are gone." Later, both of Jane's sons were restored to God through that same divine miracle.

Nothing is too difficult for God. He walks and talks with us even when we are unable to receive Him or to recognize His presence, because he does not give up on us. Our intercessory prayers remind Him of His promises.

As we mature in intercessory prayer, we understand more clearly that God acts *foremost* for *His* eternal purposes. Whatever way He answers our prayers, we are assured that they will be rooted in His eternal purposes, not just our problems. His ultimate purposes are (1) the glory of His name (see Exod. 3:15; 9:16) and (2) the establishment of His kingdom (see Ps. 145:13; Matt. 6:10). As we spend time with Him and know Him better, we'll recognize more clearly the unfolding of His purposes and His plans.

Psalm 25:12-14 says, "Who is the man that fears the LORD? Him shall He teach in the way He chooses. He himself shall dwell in prosperity, and his descendants shall inherit the earth. The secret of the LORD is with those who fear Him, and He will show them His covenant." Trust that the Lord does have a plan and that you will come to know what it is.

Sometimes we pray for an erring son or daughter and feel our prayers are going nowhere, but I assure you, our prodigals are coming home to the Father's house. When God's purpose, plan and destiny for each person connect with His perfect timing, He realigns the lost one, and suddenly, like the Prodigal Son "who came to himself," he or she turns toward home. Pray for more of these miracles!

Love and Laughter was a group of ordinary women with an extraordinary passion to know God and His ways better through the gifts of the Holy Spirit. As we prayed week after week, He answered our prayers and our faith grew. We were learning prayer principles together in the trenches, interceding for each other, for our families and friends, His Church, our nation and for anybody who came by or called. It was God's prayer school for hungry, thirsty novices. We prayed and praised, and He did the rest.

In the past four decades, hundreds of thousands of men and women, like the Love and Laughter seekers, have gathered faithfully in homes, churches, office buildings, parks and elsewhere to pray and to grow in intercessory prayer. God is looking for intercessors who are available and teachable to partner in prayer with Him and bring forth *His* purposes and plans in our lives and in the whole Earth. Together, our prayers and worship can prop open the windows of heaven, so His light and glory will fall on our homes, our cities and all nations.

The LORD is my light and my salvation; whom shall I fear? The LORD is the strength of my life; of whom shall I be afraid? One thing I have desired of the LORD, that will I seek: that I may dwell in the house of the LORD all the days of my life, to behold the beauty of the LORD, and to inquire in His temple. For in the time of trouble He shall hide me in His pavilion; in the secret place of His tabernacle He shall hide me; He shall set me high upon a rock.

PSALM 27:1,4-5

CHAPTER 7

Homeschooled in Prayer

My family and my home life were my greatest training ground for prayer. Raising three active sons, and their father, was a first-rate school for learning in things of the Spirit. Our homes are tremendous and tough mission fields.

I love being a homemaker and a mother, and I was privileged to be able to stay at home when my sons were growing up. We always ate breakfast and dinner together and kept a welcome mat out for our sons' friends. I regularly prayed over my children's beds and rooms while they were at school or elsewhere because, even though I gave birth to them, I knew I was not finished with the travail until each was birthed into the kingdom of God. Never give up praying for your spouse and children.

Psalm 127:3-5 says, "Behold, children are a heritage from the LORD, the fruit of the womb is a reward. Like arrows in the hand of a warrior, so are the children of one's youth. Happy is the man who has his quiver full of them; they shall not be ashamed, but shall speak with their enemies in the gate."

BUILDING A FAMILY

Allow me to acquaint you with the children of *my* youth. Jim is an attorney in Houston, Texas, and his wife, Christine, who shares my love for horses, is a CPA business administrator. John is a pastor of the Presbyterian Church of the Redeemer, near Atlanta; he and his wife, Lacy, have two fine sons: Stephen, who is a student at the University of Georgia, and Michael, who is a junior at Shiloh High School, where Lacy teaches. Bob is a deputy sheriff in Jefferson County, Colorado, and he and his wife, Deirdre, have three precious children, Joel, Drew and Tara. Their father, Jim, and I thank God for a family who loves and serves Him.

Let me move back several years *before* there was a family. My courtship and marriage to Jim Byerly was a classic case of young love in the heady days after World War II. In the summer of 1950, I was fresh out of Lamar High School in Houston, Texas, when my dad sent me to Southern California to be with my sister, Jeanne, who was having her first baby. Normally a mother would do that, but our mother was unable to do so. It had been a year since I'd seen Jeanne, and seeing her was like old times when we'd been "two little girls against the world."

Tragically, Jeanne's baby was stillborn.

Friends came to the hospital to lend support, and one of them was Jim Byerly, who worked with Jeanne's husband, Bill, at Shell Oil Company. A month later Jim invited me out for a date and I went.

I stayed in California hoping to help Jeanne through her grief. I enrolled at Long Beach City College, planning to transfer the next fall to the University of Texas. But romance intervened as Jim and I began to date frequently. Two months after we met, he proposed and I accepted.

I was thrilled to think I'd finally settle into a "regular" lifestyle in one place. Jim had been born and raised in Glendale,

California, and had lived in the same house all his life. He had graduated from the University of California at Los Angeles (UCLA) and gone to work for Shell Oil in California as a chemical engineer. I liked the security of his stable life—a dramatic contrast to my nomadic childhood.

Jim and I were married on February 16, 1951. I gave up my name, my plans to attend the University of Texas and my dream of becoming a ballet dancer and stage performer. We began married life in a tiny dollhouse apartment in sunny California and I continued in college until our first son, Jim Jr., was born in the fall of 1952.

I was content, but my stable, cozy nest was about to be toppled. Two months later, Jim received a job transfer to New York city, the head office of Shell Oil. It was the beginning of our corporate nomad life: We would move 13 times in the next 19 years.

Moving in the Spirit

I was disappointed in the beginning because I had so much wanted to put down roots. Gradually, however, I began to see how every place we lived there were fresh opportunities to establish friendships. Although neither Jim nor I was walking close to God in those early years, we were always active in a church. I now can see that wherever we are, God sends people to minister to us or sends them to us, so we can minister to them.

Let me give you an example. When we moved back to Houston in 1970, I yearned to find a church home where the Holy Spirit was moving. Father Jim Ferry, who had attended my Love and Laughter home prayer meetings in New Jersey, suggested we visit the Episcopal Church of the Redeemer.

My son Jim and I attended the Redeemer one Friday night, and I soon had a hook in my heart for that fellowship.

In the 1960s and 1970s, the Episcopal Church of the Redeemer was experiencing a beautiful renewal in God. It was a New Testament apostolic church, providing a community atmosphere as well as equipping and sending leaders around the world to minister.

It was the kind of place my soul longed for. Our family began worshiping there regularly and became actively involved.

Our Houston home soon became a revolving door with spiritually needy people coming and going, many people staying a week or more with us just to attend services and training at the church. One Georgia minister brought eight young drug addicts to visit our church for healing and deliverance. It was during the time these young men were in our home that my husband, Jim, realized he needed Jesus Christ in his life. He saw all the demonic things going on with these men and the gracious love God ministered through me as they were being set free. I take no credit for this because it was simply God overflowing in my life. He will make us missionaries without our ever leaving home.

During this time in Houston, I felt privileged to be both Mary and Martha–sitting at the Master's feet, like Mary, but doing the work that had to get done, like Martha.

I remember a young addict named Marvin. When his group arrived at our home, Marvin shook with fear and did not want to come in. "He's coming off heroin," the pastor explained.

That night, as usual, we gathered around the table for dinner and fellowship. Afterward, everyone went to the family room to talk about what God was doing in his life.

Marvin hung back. "I want to help you with the dishes," he said, as he proceeded to help me clear the table, even as his withdrawal tremors continued. Then Marvin made a statement that reminded me of Christ. "I cannot talk like the other boys," he confided, nodding toward the family-room conversations. "If they (the other boys) do not make their beds, I will make them for you."

I thought, *All the others are in the family room talking about Jesus and here he is acting like Jesus.*

During the next two weeks, all eight boys, including Marvin, were baptized in our swimming pool. God was answering our prayers and healing those boys in many ways.

Sometimes God does not answer our prayers right away. Those who are praying for prodigal loved ones understand the heartache in such waiting.

Sometimes, however, God does not answer right away. Mothers, fathers and grandparents who are praying for prodigal loved ones understand the heartache in such waiting. I was also about to learn some fresh lessons about God's love versus my love.

LOVING WITH HIS LOVE

Let me tell you the story of Kay, our foster daughter. The church asked us to allow a young girl from Michigan to move into our home in Houston. Kay was 15 years old and the night her adopted father brought her to our house, he sat at our dinner table telling us all the bad things she had done. Each time I looked in her direction, she bowed her face in shame.

Our first two weeks were sheer frustration. I have to say that God showed me the shallowness of my love through my experience with Kay. As much as the Spirit and God had graced me, I had great trouble accepting Kay's behavior. I had seen powerful transforming demonstrations of the Holy Spirit in many people, but nothing seemed to touch Kay. I had been praying, but I did not see the change in her that I wanted. It seemed to me that God never worked on her, but I knew He was working on me, or more specifically my heart attitude.

He was saying to me, "She has to measure up to a certain standard before you can accept her." I kept praying and trying and God finally began to say to me, "You are almost there—loving her enough for her to come to Me."

This was difficult. God had shown me judgments in myself I did not like. When I tried to explain to Jim, he was frustrated, "What do you mean it is *us*?" he would say. We had never faced anything like this with our three sons, who were good students and behaved well.

"Jim, we are not loving her with a pure love. We love her according to the standard by which we reared our children and they obeyed. Kay does not obey that standard."

She came from a horrendous background. I longed to take her under my wing because her life reminded me of my own chaotic early life. While I eagerly responded when our pastor asked Jim and me to be her foster parents, Kay had no love for us.

Still, God was saying to me, "You do not have *My* love. My love will break that wall."

"Father," I cried in desperation, "I do not know how to do this."

Still, we muddled on with Kay testing us at ever higher limits, our discipline attempts failing at every step of the way. Was God using failure to remind me of my need for total dependence on Him? Was He teaching me that compassion and humility are the heart of intercession?

"Okay, God, what do I do now?"

He had more to teach me. "If she is ever going to trust Me, she will have to trust you. She has been betrayed, molested and abused," He told me. She had little experience with trust.

One Friday night after a church service, we found Kay in the bushes outside the church with a pastor's son. I was embarrassed and angry. *This is the end for me*, I thought. *I am not going to put up with another second of this.*

Then, quietly, gently, God said, "Love her."

Things got worse. The next night, when Kay returned home from a date, she was drunk and sick, but I sat up with her as she vomited. My son Bob came to see what was wrong, and I told him she was drunk. The next morning when I saw Kay, she was in a rage.

"Why did you tell Bob I was drunk?" she demanded.

"Because that's the truth, Kay," I said.

"Truth, truth, truth–I never tell the truth," she retorted.

I looked her directly in the eye. "Kay," I said, "you have just told the truth."

She started laughing and the impenetrable wall between us began to crumble. Slowly, she drew closer to our family.

When she finally said, "I believe I am ready to accept Jesus Christ as my Savior," I thought, *God, your love is real!*

I continued to pray for guidance and wisdom and the Holy Spirit began to show me things about Kay I had not seen before. For example, when she first met people, she instinctively withdrew from them, unable to trust friendship or love offered from anyone outside our family.

When a Houston doctor asked us to take a precious newborn black baby into our home, the entire family, including Kay, rallied around and loved him. We had him for one month before a family adopted him and, during that time, I sang and prophesied over him. "David," I would say, "you will be God's king one day, so love Him and serve Him in every way." Kay would laugh and say, "You really believe that, don't you?"

I believe God used baby David, too, to demonstrate His love to Kay. She saw this baby, helpless and unable to do anything for himself, having a family rally around and love him.

I began to see Kay with new eyes of love–more like Jesus saw her. God was giving me new eyesight.

Then, another miracle seemed to happen. Kay asked us if we would adopt her, so she could live with us permanently.

Hallelujah, I thought, *We have achieved a gold mine.* We would have a daughter.

But it was not to be.

When Kay called her adoptive parents in Michigan, they refused her request to allow our family to adopt her and wired her a ticket the following day with instructions to return to Michigan immediately. She left us without being totally healed, and although she felt she was strong enough to go home, I knew there would be rough days ahead for her.

With sadness, I mailed all her things to her. When I tried to call her, I discovered the family had changed the phone number. We have never heard from Kay, but we haven't given up hope since she left in 1973 that someday our paths will cross again.

My family is resolved that whatever God enabled us to sow into Kay's life could come forth as pure gold, and I still pray that it does. We know that He does not forget our prayers.

Being a Neighborhood Lighthouse

Our neighborhoods are also our prayer responsibility. When Jesus summed up the Ten Commandments, He started with two priorities: Love God with all your heart, mind and strength, and love your neighbor as yourself.

God places us in neighborhoods to be a beacon of light to draw those who live near us to Christ. Every place we moved (and that's a lot of places), my neighborhood was my prime prayer and blessing target. I started prayer walking my neighborhoods in the early 1980s, and still do it today when I'm at home.

Whatever season of life you're in now, your home turf is your prime praying ground. If you're a grandparent, pray for your seed and your seed's seed. Remember that generational inheritance is passed down. If you are a single man or woman, you are of great value to God—Jesus was single, and look at the depth of His ministry. Allow God to show you those you are to pray for. Targeted prayers have the best effect on the lives of those who do not know Jesus, as well as those who need to grow in Him.

I like what intercessor Alice Smith says: If we're faithful to intercede for our family, neighbors, pastors and local church, God eventually will trust us with greater spiritual authority.

Each of us needs an intercessor to stand with us before God's throne in prayer. We are filling the bowls of heaven with our prayers, where they remain before God; and one day those bowls will be tipped and flow as a blessing to the earth.

And He has made from one blood every nation of men to dwell on all the face of the earth, and has determined their preappointed times and the boundaries of their dwellings.

ACTS 17:26

CHAPTER 8

The Secret Place

When I lived in New Orleans during the 1980s, God began to speak to me about my noisy heart. It is impossible to nurture silence in a noisy heart, He would reveal to me.

Today, I understand the phrase: "Be still, and know," as His Word tells us (Ps. 46:10). "Be still," He says, because He wants to share His secrets with us. "The LORD confides in those who fear him" (Ps. 25:14, *NIV*). What an awesome promise, but secrets are shared in quiet. Therefore, the discipline of silence, I have learned, is imperative if we truly want to get to know God.

LEARNING TO "BE STILL"

My life and heart were noisy with busyness in my New Orleans home. I had a son in high school and two in college, a big house and a husband who worked long hours. Although I was involved in many church and community activities and the things I was doing were good, Jesus impressed upon my heart that I needed Him alone to be the central focus of my daily life. I was missing out on the intimacy and power He wanted me to have because the Holy Spirit had to compete with dozens of other things commanding my attention. I felt strongly that He wanted me to spend time regularly with just Him in silence.

I created a prayer closet for myself, a secret place to meet with Him. I set a time and a place that was private for me, and I made a steady habit of going to that place, which was actually a special chair, and sitting there faithfully every day. I still do this, but in my new home, I have a "real" prayer closet under my stairwell—it is my favorite room in the house. I always get up earlier than my family to give myself private time, even if it's only 30 minutes alone with God.

I love reading the psalms, so in the beginning of learning about the "secret place," I often started that way. When I came into His presence, there was no prayer agenda or list. He met me there, and my ability or inability to adequately pray did not limit Him. In this daily quiet time and place, God began shifting my focus off me and my wants and needs and onto Him. He was raising my prayer life to a new level.

I witnessed the same changes happening across the country as more intercessors took to their prayer closets for daily communion with God. When we came together to pray and fellowship, in small groups, at conferences or large worship gatherings, miracles happened. We were seeing as never before, that the very things we had asked for in our prayer closets were being miraculously released into our lives in abundance (see Heb. 11:6).

In a lifetime of prayer and intercession, I have spent more time in my secret chamber than any other place. We tend to think that public or corporate praying is the most important kind of praying. It is powerful, but God has taught us that the quality and quantity of our private praying greatly impacts the power of our public praying. I believe what happens in our secret prayer life is a key that unlocks heaven for us as God sends forth His ministry of intercession when we are on our knees.

I believe what happens in our secret prayer life is a key that unlocks heaven for us. In my secret place of prayer He intensifies my passion for Him.

In my secret place, He intensifies my passion for Him. The more I learn about His character, the more I yearn to know Him more deeply and make Him known to others. In prayer my spirit echoes the words of the psalmist, "My soul longs, yes, even faints for the courts of the LORD; my heart and my flesh cry out for the living God" (Ps. 84:2).

Learning to Listen

The discipline of my fellowship with Christ is in silence, solitude, surrender and serenity. As I enter my prayer closet, I try to surrender all my thoughts to God, as I concentrate on being like Mary, who sat at Christ's feet to learn from Him, and I resist my Martha tendency to be distracted. I don't want to worry about what will happen in this time or be burdened by what will be accomplished here. I simply desire to receive His thoughts and to pray His prayers, not mine. When I am still and silent before Him, He gives me the substance and direction for my time of prayer.

Often God directs me to pray for people or situations I would not have thought of on my own. We are intercessors sometimes for people who never know it. In fact, we may not know why we are led to pray for a certain person or situation until later. And, there are instances when God sends us an "emergency alert"– what intercessors call an SOS from God.

One such morning as I sat quietly, I felt an urgency in my spirit to pray for my pastor's physical protection.

"God, send ministering angels to surround Him right now and spare His life," I prayed, guided by the Holy Spirit, but not understanding what might be happening to my pastor. It was an hour before I felt this burden lifted and I resumed my prayers.

Later that day, my pastor phoned.

"I wondered if the intercessors prayed for me this morning," he started.

"Let me tell you what I prayed," I jumped in. "God interrupted my prayer time this morning to pray specifically for you. I'm sure other intercessors did, too."

Then he told me his story.

"A man came into my office this morning and pointed a gun at my head. He said that if I did what he said, he wouldn't harm me. He led me around at gunpoint while he robbed the church. Before he left, I invited him to come again, without a gun, because I had something better to give him than silver Communion trays and candlesticks."

The incident happened at the very hour when the Lord interrupted my prayer time with His SOS. We must be sensitive to hear the gentle, quiet voice of the Lord and remember the words of Isaiah 65:24: "It shall come to pass that before they call, I will answer; and while they are still speaking, I will hear."

Prayer begins with God, seeps into our hearts and gives us the courage to ask for what God is ready to give–not what we want at the moment. At these times, our requests are more consistent with His will. We must remember that praying is not about getting God's attention–the purpose of prayer is to focus our attention upon Him.

He will, in different ways, show us a picture or communicate to us His purposes. It seems that some people's prayers aim at "nothing," and that is exactly what they hit, causing them to get discouraged with praying. When we pray focused prayers, we are seeking God's face and we will not miss His heart. It takes focused prayers to hit the mark.

Inside the Prayer Closet

As I wait in silence or pray, I often feel a flutter inside my body—sometimes my heart seems to beat a little faster. I have learned to know and recognize this as the gentleness of the Holy Spirit present with me as He begins to pray His yearnings through me. I am in His secret place, which is His presence: "In the shelter of your presence you hide them" (Ps. 31:20, *NIV*). His love, joy and peace fill my heart in the serenity of His closeness.

At times, I fall on the floor and begin weeping over my sins and the sins that have so devastated our nation; or I sit quietly, learning to recognize His still small voice. Other times, I even imagine crawling upon His lap, for He is my Abba (Daddy), and He lifts me up.

I love corporate prayer and worship, but God has made my prayer-closet experiences the most satisfying and effective times of my life. As I bow before Him, sensing His presence, He reveals His heart and I am caught up into the heavenlies where multiple facets of His character are revealed.

It is during this time of touching heaven that He touches Earth through us, like electricity through conductors—then His restoration and healing flow.

I believe we must spend time every day in prayer and worship honoring God. Then, when Jesus Christ's extravagant love flows through us, it is the greatest gift the Church has to give to a lost world.

Sadly, the Church has not accomplished this mission. We have been so busy doing the "works of Christ" that we have failed to spend time pursuing Him intimately–His foremost desire! I ponder how we can move from the busyness of our hectic world to a place of shelter and refuge in Christ for when we abide in the "secret place of the Most High God," and He transforms by His transcendent beauty, the world will be drawn to Jesus.

The gospel is veiled from those who don't know Christ (see 2 Cor. 4:3-4). They see Him, His beauty and love, only when these are reflected through us, His earthen vessels.

My friend Barbara Clark says, "Who we are in the secret place with our Lord is who we are on the public byways of the world." If we neglect a private prayer life in intercession with God, then we have nothing to give outside to others.

I am reminded of the Old Testament priests assigned to go into the Holy of Holies and come out and tell what they heard from God, morning, noon and night. Living on this side of the Cross, we are all called to priestly intercession for His Church. Spending time alone with Him helps us develop a full and satisfying prayer life and ministry to the Lord. When we spend time in His presence, it changes us to reflect *His* heart and beauty–and be assured, the world will notice the difference.

God has blessed me with an insatiable desire to pursue and to know Him intimately. If you do not yet have this passion, the Bible says to ask for it: "Draw near to God and He will draw near to you" (Jas. 4:8). Pray this verse and expect it to happen, because we know it is the desire of *His* heart.

Contemplative Prayer with Present and Past

In recent years, I have experienced another form of prayer I love that I discovered through Bonnie Shannonhouse's prayer booklet entitled *The Lost Coin—The Little Hours,* which is based upon the medieval *Book of Hours*. Bonnie writes from Psalm 55:17:

> Evening and Morning, and at Noon, I will pray and cry aloud and He shall hear my voice. "The kingdom of heaven," Jesus said, "is like a lost coin. The woman searched for it diligently until it was found. What woman having ten silver coins, if she loses one, does not light a lamp and sweep the house and seek diligently until she finds it. When she has found it, she calls together her friends and neighbors saying, 'Rejoice with me for I have found the coin which I had lost' "(Luke 15:8-9).[1]

During biblical times, a woman's dowry often consisted of gold and silver coins. She would sew them onto her headdress as adornment or wear them as jewelry, because only personal apparel of a woman was considered her property. These few coins might well have been her only source of wealth and material security, so every coin was precious.

Bonnie writes, "We have lost one of the most valuable coins of our spiritual life—the inclination to constant prayer and the discipline of coming at fixed times during the day before the Lord who is our source of wealth and security."[2]

Presbyterian Church founder John Calvin reminds us, "To prayer are we indebted for penetrating to those riches which are treasured up for us with our heavenly Father."[3]

The key to reaching the treasured riches, Bonnie says, is intercession. As a devout Jew, Jesus would have prayed daily: an example worthy to be followed. Being raised by Mary and Joseph, who would have followed the devout practices of the day, Jesus would have followed the same custom of praying at the fixed hourly prayer times of the Temple services observed in Jerusalem.

When I've stayed at Christ Church in Israel's Old City of Jerusalem, the chimes *still* ring at nine, noon and three, calling believers to pray. Jesus gave us the opportunity of choosing a new spiritual birth, and with that comes the challenge of walking in His ways, hourly.

Calvin said, "Zeal for the Kingdom and Glory of God ought not to seize us by starts, but urge us without intermission so that every time should appear seasonable."[4]

The habit of daily disciplined prayer has been abandoned by all but the most devout Christians. In its place, we have substituted "a moment's thought with God" before starting or ending our day.

In the late 1990s, I began traveling with Bonnie to different cities and cathedrals for an interdenominational Day of Prayer. I saw again so clearly what I had seen in the 1960s, 1970s and 1980s—the desire of the Father heart of God to woo His Church to come *first* to Him, that we might experience His entire blazing splendor. As we see Him as He is, He then, by an act of His grace, develops His magnificent character in us.

Daily prayer takes time and discipline. When daily communion with God is deeply embedded within us, we will do many things differently, starting with how we treat each other. We will fellowship in the pure love of Christ. Instead of seeing our differences, we will seek ways to walk in unity.

I do not follow the teachings of *The Lost Coin* as a religious ritual; rather, I follow them because I want to further explore the depth and width of praying with other Christians around the world at the same hours of the day. My daily prayer times are set at nine, noon and three. As I read these writings from the Bible and the thoughts and meditations of others upon them, I find myself warmed by the presence of Jesus and His love.

If we seek this "lost coin" of disciplined daily prayer, God promises that we and our children shall find the coin of exceptional worth—a wealth of biblical truth that will bring us into His presence. God's words repeated daily seal into our hearts and minds His precepts, statutes and commandments. They become our guideposts in a world otherwise without direction or moral focus.

Called to Be a House of Prayer

For years now, my heart has been a house of prayer. I joyfully serve God this way. First Corinthians 3:16 says, "Do you not know that you are the temple of God and that the Spirit of God dwells in you?"

Yes, I know my body houses the Holy Spirit. I believed the deep yearnings that come from within me are from the Holy Spirit, and I believe the Church worldwide is called to be a house of prayer for all nations. God has erected His tabernacle, or temple, in our hearts. And who is the Church but believers who will honor and worship God in their temples?

God has called us, individually and collectively, to be a house of prayer. Prayer and intercession are a wonderful way to experience God. The keys to doing this are a secret place, a quiet time and an expectant heart.

Even them I will bring to My holy mountain, and make them joyful in My house of prayer . . . for all nations. The Lord GOD, who gathers the outcasts of Israel, says, "Yet I will gather to him others besides those who are gathered to him."

ISAIAH 56:7-8

CHAPTER 9

Building Faith Muscles

In God's history book, these are exciting times to be alive, as increased prayer and intercession push open heaven's gates so the glory and power of God can flood the earth. The prayer warriors of Aglow International, together with other praying women, have played a big part in the miraculous move of God's Spirit that we're witnessing at this juncture in history.

I spent 20 glorious years with the Aglow ministry, building faith muscles by praying and working alongside an army of women who take their faith to the front lines every day. My association with Aglow started with a divine intervention, starring a cast of fish (yes, the real things). Here's some history.

In 1967, God raised up Aglow to be a brand-new ministry for women in America. Aglow's ministry derives its name comes from Romans 12:11: "Never lag in zeal and in earnest endeavor; be aglow and burning with the Spirit, serving the Lord" (*AMP*). Our fellowship meetings were Holy Spirit-led for women from all denominations.

When I was first asked to become a part of Aglow in 1977, I said no. I had just finished leading a year of prayer for the city of New Orleans, working with pastors and priests there, so I was reluctant to become involved in a women's organization. Then I had a divine visitation.

One day, when I was running by Lake Pontchartrain in Metairie, Louisiana, I asked God to give me a sign or word if I was to join this new organization being formed in Louisiana. Finishing my jog, I sat on a big rock overlooking the lake and prayed for guidance. Within moments, I began to notice fish jumping wildly in Lake Pontchartrain—there were big fish, little fish and fish of all colors. The number of fish was so great that a fisherman on the nearby bank was using a net instead of a rod to catch them.

"O Lord," I marveled, "this is like the New Testament Church."

As I watched the leaping fish, I became aware that God might be speaking to me. "Father, are You showing me something in this great demonstration that I have never seen in my life?" I asked. Then I saw a fisherman in a boat lower a net and bring in a haul of fish. "Lord," I said, "that is like You with Your disciples, telling them to throw their net on the other side; then they started catching a haul of fish."

This is what I believe God said to me that day and why I became involved with Aglow ministry: "There are hidden, hurting women all over the city of New Orleans not seen by you, or by the churches, but seen by Me. Aglow is a net of My love to draw the hidden, hurting women to Myself."

God gave me the go-ahead signal for Aglow and started unfolding another chapter in His plans and purposes in my life. Do you know that He has a special purpose for *your* life, too?

"You were given life by God to be a woman of destiny and to impact the lives around you," says Cindy Jacobs, in her book *Women of Destiny*. In order to do that, she says, you must discover God's purposes for your life and fulfill them to the best of your ability.[1]

Through the ages, God has used ordinary women to extraordinarily influence their families, churches, cities and nations. He may have different purposes for different seasons of our lives, and some of us, says Cindy, "have bigger mountains to climb and greater challenges to overcome than others. Fortunately, it's not what you have, but Whom you know that makes the difference!"[2]

Romans 8:28 tells us, "And we know that all things work together for good to those who love God, to those who are the called according to His purpose." If we study this verse carefully, says Cindy, "we see that things work together for good to those who have 'the anchor of purpose.' All things may not be working together for good because we are aimless and don't know our purpose (in Him). We could interchange the word 'purpose' for 'destiny.'"[3]

An Army of Praying Women

God knows the destiny business well. My Aglow assignment suited me just fine. Ours is a ministry of prayer, worship and evangelism–things I love. Aglow has also been a leadership training tool in the hand of God, raising up many modern-day Esthers, Deborahs, Ruths, Annas and others for "such a time as this." He sovereignly used this ministry first in America and then in more than 160 nations of the world. Now, like a rippling lake, millions of women who have received ministry through Aglow fellowships are reaching out to others.

I worked as an Aglow leader several years in Louisiana until I was asked to serve on the International Board of Directors. Aglow had been growing at a phenomenal rate. In 1972, 60 fellowships were meeting monthly around the United States, and by the late 1970s, there were 800 fellowships on four continents. In Louisiana, our local Aglow fellowships were seeing 30 to 60 women a month come to Christ. My own Aglow area board started 22 local fellowships in 18 months. It was an exciting time—it was God's time, and He was moving mightily in women's lives.

In 1982, I invited Jane Hansen, Aglow International president, to speak at our Louisiana retreat. During her stay, she and I spent hours sharing ministry stories and dreams. We believed it was God's plan in this hour for the woman to be cojoined, or reconciled, with the man in order to possess the full inheritance of God and fulfill God's plan as stated in Genesis—that the male and female *together* subdue the entire Earth. God had given the same revelation to Jane, to me and to a dear friend, Marilyn Quirk. When the three of us talked, it was like a fountain of water gushing forth through each of us, giving life to each of us as we shared the revelations of God.

Marilyn later was an instrument God used to start The Magnificat, a Catholic women's organization, and Jane became a close friend as we prayed and ministered together many times. The hand of God put us together, as I truly believe God ordains some friendships for His supernatural purposes. I remember my friend and mentor Joy Dawson teaching me about covenantal friendships. Joy was a speaker at a 1981 conference in Buffalo, New York. When I waved to her as I walked by the platform, she called me aside and then motioned Jane off the platform. We stood close as Joy shared that she believed God had brought the three of us together for His strategic purposes, which would be fulfilled as we experienced the love and unity that Jesus prayed we would share with each other (see John 17). Joy then indicated that I would be like an armor bearer to Jane. The dictionary defines "armor" as "a defensive covering, a safeguard or protection." The Bible says that one of the things intercessors do is build up a wall of protection in time of battle (see Ezek. 13:4-5). I watched and prayed as God raised Jane to new heights, and new nations came into the Aglow ministry.

In 1993, I accepted a request by Aglow International's board of directors to serve as the U.S. national president. "You are to be a voice for God across America," was the prophetic word they spoke to me. I honored this call by moving from Houston, Texas, to the state of Washington, knowing that God had a strategic role for Aglow in His eternal plans and that He would fill me with new vision and strategies to energize Aglow in America.

It is not difficult to see how desperately the poor and ravaged parts of our cities need God's healing touch. The compassionate heart of Jesus wants to reside in these places.

He led us out to minister in the streets of cities in the United States and throughout the world. Prayer was the spark that lit the fuse and kept it glowing. Aglow's network of praying, warring women had prayer leaders in all 50 states and in many other nations, a powerful force interceding for the ministry and for the evangelization of the women of the world.

In the United States we saw His hand upon Aglow's call to evangelization–to do acts of kindness and deeds of love in our neighborhoods. We started lighthouses of prayer before the term was well known. We expanded our prison ministry and prayer-blitzed cities large and small.

One of my great privileges was to lead Aglow's outreach to the inner cities across America and watch how God impacted them. The wonderful and gifted Mary Willette walked beside me in this ministry, and local and area Aglow officers were vital boosters. It is not difficult to see how desperately the poor and ravaged parts of our cities need God's healing touch. The compassionate heart of Jesus wants to reside in these places as we read in Psalm 34:18 (*NIV*), "The LORD is close to the broken-hearted and saves those who are crushed in spirit." He was calling Aglow women to step out of our comfort zones and take His heart to the streets and to His forgotten people.

Let me tell you about an Aglow mission trip to Washington, D.C.'s inner city in 1996. The first night, we hosted a dinner for the city's pastors and the next morning met with Lloyd Ogilvie, chaplain of the U.S. Senate. Then we took to the streets for a prayer blitz.

As we passed out brochures inviting people to a free lunch and "a day of outdoor fun," many said they were afraid to come to the square where we planned the event. One woman scanned the brochure, soberly stared at me and said, "That square is a Vietnam," she said. "I don't go there. Twelve people were shot there last Saturday."

We did not want to presume on God's grace, but we knew He had called us to the inner city and that He would protect us. We had a large attendance. We served pizza and entertained children and adults with concerts and drama skits. By the end of the day many people had given their lives to Christ.

I remember another city outreach, when we served lunch and testified about the transforming love of Jesus. After we finished, 20 women walked forward and dumped drugs and cigarettes from their purses and asked Jesus into their lives. After the party, four policemen who had watched the event from the second floor of the recreation hall came down and thanked us for what we had done in their city–two of them then accepted Christ as their Savior.

When God's Church abandoned America's cities and moved to the suburbs, we left Satan a claim to dominate the cities. I believe God used Aglow to sow seeds in those desperate places during the past decade, and now we are seeing those seeds come to life. I praise God that He is raising up more Holy Spirit-empowered soldiers to take back our inner cities in Jesus' name.

THE DAYS OF GOD'S "SUDDENLIES"

I will always carry the ministry of Aglow in my heart, being ever mindful that 59 percent of the people living today see the world through the eyes of a woman. As I've traveled to many nations, I've witnessed women living in dire poverty and unspeakable distress. I've listened and shared, cried and counseled with hurting, wounded women in all walks of life. While their physical and material needs differ greatly, their internal needs are the same. They all long for some affection, attention, approval and acceptance. And they all need Jesus.

The last verse of Isaiah 60 says, "A little one shall become a thousand, and the small one a strong nation. I, the LORD, will hasten it in its time."

I believe we are living in the days of God's "suddenlies." If we continue to pray and seek His face, He will pour out His miracles upon His people, that we might be a bright, shining light to this nation and other nations of the world.

Remember what I wrote earlier about God-ordained friendships? The joy of my heart was to work with the seven women who served with me on the U.S. national board of Algow, and I love each of them deeply. I will always be grateful to God for raising up the Aglow ministry and allowing me to be a small part in His purposes and plans.

In 1997, the leaders of Promise Keepers gave Jane Hansen and me each an engraved plaque honoring Aglow International for "30 years of faithful service to the Lord and loving ministry to women worldwide." This salute belongs equally to the hundreds of thousands of Aglow women and other praying women who every day take their faith to the front lines. The other words engraved on the plaque are echoed in the book of Micah, and they are *my* prayer for praying women everywhere: May the Lord continue to enlarge the place of your tent as you carry His heart of mercy, compassion and reconciliation to the hurting women throughout the earth.

I beseech you therefore, brethren, by the mercies of God, that you present your bodies a living sacrifice, holy, acceptable to God, which is your reasonable service. And do not be conformed to this world, but be transformed by the renewing of your mind, that you may prove what is that good and acceptable and perfect will of God. For I say, through the grace given to me, to everyone who is among you, not to think of himself more highly than he ought to think, but to think soberly, as God has dealt to each one a measure of faith. For as we have many members in one body, but all the members do not have the same function, so we, being many, are one body in Christ, and individually members of one another.

ROMANS 12:1-5

CHAPTER 10

Divine Appointments in Daily Life

Miracles often are a daily affair when we have a "praying life" instead of a separate "prayer life." A praying life allows the Holy Spirit, who has taken up permanent residence in us, to lead us to people who are hurting and in need. Jesus sent us the Holy Spirit to help us pray what is on the Father's heart. Our job is to listen and recognize His leading.

I like how Jennifer Kennedy Dean, executive director of the Praying Life Foundation, describes this praying life.

> [It] is a dimension of living, in which you experience minute-by-minute the flow of God's provision. You are met at every step with the progressive unfolding of His tailor-made plan for your life. Ephesians 2:10 says, "For we are His workmanship, created in Christ Jesus for good works, which God prepared beforehand that we should walk in them." You cease your struggle to find the

> will of God because the will of God has found you. Living life open to the Spirit—actively and intentionally cooperating with God on an everyday basis—is possible. Jesus showed the way . . .[1]

Almost every day, I find myself involved in unexpected Spirit-appointed tasks as God points out troubled people everywhere who need an intercessor to plead their case in heaven's court. I am honored and thrilled the Father entrusts me with His precious ones. In prayer and practice, we learn to recognize His voice and His leading. He books divine appointments for us; He opens the doors; and He will do it in unexpected times and places.

Intercessors are empowered by the Holy Spirit to discern the clashing of the kingdom of God and the kingdom of darkness. Philippians 4:6 states, "Be anxious for nothing, but in everything by prayer and supplication, with thanksgiving, let your requests be made known to God." I take great confidence in this verse.

Unexpected Mission Fields

I travel thousands of miles a year as an intercessor and speaker, so I spend lots of time in cars and airplanes. They are often a mission field for miraculous encounters.

I remember a few surprise appointments while flying home after an Aglow prayer blitz in Miami, Florida. I had recently become the U.S. national president of Aglow and was traveling with a board member and friend, Ruth. By God's grace we were bumped into first class, and as we were waiting for takeoff, the flight attendant asked if we wanted something to drink. When she walked away, Ruth whispered to me, "Bobbye, I sense this woman is disturbed. Since you are on the aisle, when she returns, read Psalm 121 to her." The attendant came back to our seats, and I asked her permission to read something especially for her. She agreed.

Softly, I repeated the words of the psalm:

> I will lift up my eyes to the hills—from whence comes my help? My help comes from the LORD, who made heaven and earth. He will not allow your foot to be moved; He who keeps you will not slumber. Behold, He who keeps Israel shall neither slumber nor sleep. The LORD is your keeper; the LORD is your shade at your right hand. The sun shall not strike you by day, nor the moon by night. The LORD shall preserve you from all evil; He shall preserve your soul. The LORD shall preserve your going out and your coming in from this time forth, and even forevermore.

Tears welled up in the flight attendant's eyes, and she quickly walked away. She returned shortly, leaned over and told us quietiy, "I am an alcoholic. The words you read mean so much to me right now."

Later on, the flight attendant walked back to see us once again. She commented that the pilot of our plane did not like her, which made her job much harder. Sensing we needed to pray, I said, "May we pray with you briefly?"

The three of us walked quietly to the tiny kitchen area in the front, and she closed the curtain behind us. Ruth and I gently, lovingly prayed prayers of deliverance over her and spoke blessings into her life.

Later, after we were back in our seats, we noticed the pilot walk out and say something to her. Ruth and I immediately prayed. The flight attendant then walked down the aisle with a smile on her face, leaned over and whispered, "He complimented me and said I was doing a good job."

Excited by what had just happened, I wrote out Psalm 121 on the back of an Aglow booklet entitled *Receive All God Has for You* and gave it to the flight attendant. She said she would read it and thanked us for our prayers and encouragement. As we left the airplane, she gave each of us a hug and said, "I feel better than I have felt in weeks."

I was grateful Ruth followed the Holy Spirit's prompting and asked me to read that psalm to this troubled woman. Ministering to her had been a divine appointment arranged by God—and a powerful reminder that helping in the healing process of every person's soul, claiming or reclaiming it for the Lord and for His kingdom is the first chapter in God's miracle book. Sometimes this happens in prayer services or in large crusades, but it also can happen in an airplane galley.

On another trip, a flight attendant saw me reading my Bible and asked if I was a Christian. She smiled and said, "I am also a Christian."

"Thanks for sharing that good news with me," I told her.

Midway into the flight, she came and sat in a vacant seat across the aisle, and leaned over to speak to me quietly. "I am a Christian, but I am so depressed," she confessed. "I am not supposed to talk to passengers about personal things, but since you are still reading your Bible, maybe you can help me. I was despondent enough last Friday that I attempted suicide again."

I started praying silently: "OK, Lord, what shall I do next?"

We moved to empty seats at the back of the plane and began to talk. With the Holy Spirit giving me words, I prayed quietly with her, binding the spirit of murder and suicide. Then I reminded her about God's holy, unconditional love, telling her, "You do not have to be fearful, because God is more powerful than the enemy who is seeking to destroy you." As I was talking of His love for her she began to weep. We talked awhile longer, and she recommitted her life to Jesus.

I should tell you that I don't attempt to convert everyone I sit next to on airplanes. I chat with those who want to make small talk, and many times I just read. But if God gives me an open door, I walk through it. I listen and try to discern what is happening in each situation, and fortunately I care deeply about people.

I should tell you that I don't attempt to convert everyone I meet. But if God gives me an open door, I walk through it.

Sometimes these appointments don't go so smoothly, but God does have a sense of humor. Let me tell you about the time when there was no room in the inn.

On my way to speak at a retreat, I had to change planes three times in order to reach my destination. When one flight was delayed, I missed all the connecting ones, so I had to phone my hostess to tell her I wouldn't arrive until after midnight. I could hear the fear in her voice as she said she did not drive that late in the evening.

"Oh! Then I will find a hotel near the airport," I responded. That was easier said than done!

I arrived to find every available room within miles occupied by athletes practicing for the Winter Olympics. I finally found a seat and settled in at the airport for the night. About 2 A.M., an airport guard advised me the terminal was closing and I would have to go outside. *He can't be serious*, I thought. "Can you just lock me inside? I have not been able to get a hotel room. I need to stay here until morning," I implored.

"Sorry, but no," he answered. So, I lugged my suitcase outside to the curb and sat on it. *Okay, Lord, what now?* I thought.

Shortly, a young man drove up and asked if I needed help. After introducing ourselves, I told Tom my plight.

"Maybe if I take you to one of the hotels, they will let you in if you are standing there," Tom commented.

So off we went in Tom's car. I was turned away at two hotels, and then we were given the name of a third place with a possible vacancy. Tom indicated he did not think I would want to stay there.

"It's three o'clock in the morning, and you have no place to stay. How can you still be smiling?" he asked, as we returned to the car. "Son, I am here on the Lord's assignment, and I have to trust He knows what He is doing. I believe He sent you to be a comfort to me."

Tom started weeping. He told me that his father was a pastor but confessed, "I left the Lord and haven't been in church for years."

He pulled his car to the side of the road, and we talked for the next 40 minutes. Tom recommitted his life to Christ.

I thought, *Lord, this is why I am here—for this young man—yet I still have no place to go.*

I told Tom to take me to the "mystery hotel" the last clerk had mentioned. He acted nervous but agreed.

"How long will you need the room?" the motel's female clerk asked me.

"About three hours," I said naively.

Tom carried my luggage, walked me to my room and said good-bye. As he was leaving, I spoke blessings over him.

It did not take me long to realize I was in a house of prostitution—the walls were very thin.

Early the following morning, I went to the office looking for a cup of coffee.

"None here," said the man at the desk. "But you can get a cup at the bar three blocks down the street."

"I do not frequent bars," I replied.

"Are you the woman who checked in a few hours ago?" he asked curiously. "My wife told me about you."

As we talked, he smoked two cigarettes and started coughing severely. I kept feeling impressed to pray for this man.

"Sir, may I pray for you? It is not God's will that you have emphysema. Smoking these cigarettes is not healthy for you." He agreed for me to pray, but I could sense he was nervous. I put my hand on his shoulder and started praying. As God touched him, he crumpled to the floor and lay very still, his eyes closed. The female clerk from the night before came to see what happened.

"It is okay," I assured her. "Your husband was having a severe coughing spell, and I prayed for him. I believe he is resting in the Lord."

She was astonished. I was quietly asking God what I should do next. "Be at peace," His still small voice whispered to me.

The man opened his eyes. "What did you do?" he asked. His cough had subsided.

His wife gave me a cup of coffee, and then we sat and talked.

"I thought I ended up here by accident, but now I do not believe it was an accident at all," I explained. "God wants to touch your lives with His love." He certainly did!

I phoned the retreat president and told her where I was. Aghast, she told me that she never went to that part of town. At that point I figured perhaps I should just fly home—until she said she would pick me up in 30 minutes.

God redeems everything, and this was certainly evident on that trip. The retreat itself was wonderful. As I was giving my testimony about the Japanese man asking me if I knew Jesus, a Chinese student, who had stopped to see what was going on in the auditorium, literally came running down the aisle.

"If a Japanese man helped you, would you help a Chinese man?" He fell into my arms sobbing, "I have heard you talking about Jesus, and I want Him in my life."

The 500 people at the retreat, mostly women, embraced this young man in prayer. The Holy Spirit was obviously at work in his heart.

Discipling the Body

I have also been blessed to be on the receiving end of some divine appointments in everyday life.

When I was 40 years old, my son Jim started me on a walking and jogging program that, to this day, helps keep me healthy and fit. While living in New Orleans, I walked a mile a day at first, then three miles a day, and eventually I was jogging up to five miles a day along Lake Pontchartrain. Before I walked home, I would climb onto one of the big rocks next to the lakeshore, cool off and meditate on the holy things of God. I had heard stories of crimes being committed near this lake, but I trusted God would protect me.

One time, I noticed an Orthodox rabbi walking and praying by the lake. As I passed him, I spontaneously blurted out, "Blessed be the Lord God of Israel." I kept jogging, thinking, *Why did I do that? You do not know that man. Orthodox rabbis don't talk with women on bike paths.*

When he passed me on the return, he responded without stopping, "Blessed be His holy name forever."

We didn't introduce ourselves, but this became a pattern each time I returned to the lake. As I jogged by him, I called out an Old Testament Scripture; on the return, he responded with a matching Scripture. We communicated this way for about six months.

One day, as I passed him, I said, "He welcomes us to His banqueting table."

"His banner over us is love," he responded immediately.

About a mile down the path, alone, I ran into danger. A menacing-looking man on a bicycle pushed me off the path. Knowing this could be trouble, I called upon the name of Jesus. The man laughed at me.

I heard rapid footsteps, turned around and saw a huge, beautiful black man running toward me. The menace mounted his bike and took off.

"Are you all right?" the rescuer asked. "Let me run back along the path with you so that man will not return," he offered. Then, we met the Jewish rabbi waiting on the path.

"I saw God's jogger was in trouble," he told me, "and I asked this man to help you." My rescuer, I learned, was a football player for the New Orleans Saints.

As we grow in our intimate relationship with Him, we will recognize opportunities we did not see before.

I hugged that rabbi. "Thanks be to God," I said. The rabbi and I soon developed a bond of friendship, and he shared with me the things he was teaching others.

Our job as believers and intercessors is to recognize the opportunities when God presents them to us. This includes being able to hear His prompting, which often comes in gentle ways. We must know His Word well, so we will be confident of His principles and sensitive to what is needed at the moment—an encouraging word, a loving gesture, a prayer or something more. Like the traffic controller informing the pilot what to do next, we wait for the Holy Spirit to give us guidance. We can't just rush in and bowl people over.

God will use our mind, senses and emotions to reveal who Jesus is to people He puts in our path.

How do we listen for the voice of the Lord? By being a diligent, persistent seeker after the heart and ways of God—not just a casual inquirer.

For me, this took many hours of praying, waiting and studying God's Word to learn His ways. Slowly, surely, I fell deeper in love with Him. The key was spending time with Him.

As we grow in this intimate relationship with Him, we will recognize opportunities we did not see before. We know God can operate through dramatic displays of supernatural power. But many of His miracles come in the quiet ordinariness of daily life.

My thoughts are not your thoughts, nor are your ways
My ways . . . For as the heavens are higher than the earth,
so are My ways higher than your ways, and
My thoughts than your thoughts.

ISAIAH 55:8-9

CHAPTER 11

Wells of Intimacy

For Christmas of 1993, my friend, Mary Lance Sisk, gave me a gift I treasure to this day: *Life of the Beloved* by Henri Nouwen. This book deeply impacted my life as I saw myself in a new light and it dawned on me that I am His beloved.

I had always thought of "beloved" in Scripture as applying only to Jesus. Passages such as Matthew 3:17, "Suddenly a voice came from heaven, saying, 'This is My beloved Son, in whom I am well pleased,'" were very familiar to me. But when I read this little book, I was struck with the awesome revelation that I—an ordinary, flawed woman—was *also* God's "beloved." You are, too.

Seeing ourselves as God sees us is liberating! When we anchor our identity in what He thinks of us, instead of how others judge us, that is what I call freedom.

Now, reading this book, I was being called to a simpler lifestyle as I was awakened by the simplicity of the gospel of Jesus Christ. I felt strongly that I needed to simplify my relationship with my "Beloved" through silence, surrender, solitude and serenity.

This wake-up call to simplicity came at a crucial time for me. I was an intercessor for spiritual leaders, the church, my state, my nation, plus I was starting a new ministry role as the U.S. national president of Aglow. I was superbusy, and, unfortunately, I had a lot of company—many Christian leaders were experiencing spiritual exhaustion and burnout in the 1990s.

Then I read what Henri Nouwen wrote about this predicament:

> Well, you and I don't have to kill ourselves. We are the Beloved. We are intimately loved long before our parents, teachers, spouses, children and friends loved or wounded us. That is the truth I want you to claim for yourself. That's the truth spoken by the voice that says, "You are my Beloved."[1]

Imagine reading a love letter from Jesus. Here is some of what He would say to you:

> I have called you by name, from the very beginning. You are mine, and I am yours.
>
> You are my Beloved, on you my favor rests. I have molded you in the depths of the earth and knitted you together in your mother's womb. I have carried you in the palm of my hands and hidden you in the shadow of my embrace.
>
> I look at you with infinite tenderness and care for you with a care more intimate than that of a mother for her child.
>
> I have counted every hair on your head and guided you at every step.
>
> Wherever you go, I go with you, and wherever you rest, I keep watch.

> I will give you food that will satisfy all your hunger and drink that will quench all your thirst.
>
> I will not hide my face from you. You know me as your own, as I know you as My own. You belong to me. I am your father, your mother, your brother, your sister, your lover and your spouse . . . yes, even your child . . . wherever you are I will be. Nothing will ever separate us. We are one.[2]

Henri Nouwen writes that every time we listen with great attentiveness to this voice that calls us "the beloved," we'll discover within ourselves a desire to hear that voice longer and more deeply. "It is like discovering a well in the desert. Once you have touched wet ground, you want to dig deeper."[3]

HUMILITY AND HOLINESS

Digging deeper into these wells of living water and walking more fully in the purposes of God became a priority passion for me during the decade of the 1990s. What a privilege it has been for me to be linked with God's intercessors from every state and even other nations. We have been prayer pilgrims together. An increasing number of intercessors have joined with me since 1990, when Peter Wagner asked me to raise up intercessors for the Spiritual Warfare Network and later the United Prayer Track.

I know this journey in intercession must be walked in humility and holiness before God and before the Body of Christ. Hebrews 12:14 says, "Pursue peace with all people, and holiness, without which no one will see the Lord." This awesome thought about the importance of holiness is in the Bible to urge us to draw closer to Him.

This holiness will flow from a walk of humility. Andrew Murray says, "Humility is perfect quietness of heart. It is to be at rest when nobody praises me, and when I am blamed and despised." Humility is not the crushing of self, but the liberating of self. Without humility, we will not yield to God's desire to cleanse, heal, redeem and restore us.

Humility is not the crushing of self but the liberating of self. Without humility, we will not yield to God's desire to cleanse, heal, redeem and restore us.

God made us to be partakers of His holiness as we endure His divine chastening. I have been scolded by God many times for my own disobedience. He loves us, but He honors His own ways. Refusing His chastening robs us of His holiness and can rob our children and their children's children of blessings. Do we want our children to inherit spiritual DNA that has been not been purified by God?

I like Brian J. Bailey's illustration of this phenomenon. While speaking at an Aglow Fellowship meeting in New Zealand, he shared a vision God gave him: "I saw three generations. I saw the grandmother with a tiny weed in her heart. I saw the mother with a bush in her heart. Then I saw the daughter, and that bush had become a mighty tree within her heart that was dominating her life."

The Lord spoke very clearly, said Brian. If the grandmother had only allowed that weed to be taken out of her heart, it would never have been passed on from generation to generation. Unfortunately, with each passing generation, these weeds become stronger.

God paid the price for our sins by sending His Son, Jesus, who never sinned, to die for our sins and thus satisfy His own wrath toward us. This simply means that God, at the Cross, treated Jesus as though He had committed our sins, even though He was righteous. On the other hand, when we believe in Christ, the Father treats us as though we were as righteous and holy as Christ: "For He made Him who knew no sin to be sin for us, that we might become the righteousness of God in [Christ]" (2 Cor. 5:21).

God has put into our spiritual account the very worth of Christ, through His atoning blood, shed on the cross. Sadly, there are many Christians who are unaware of this great, inexhaustible account, while others simply refuse to believe that such an abundant blessing belongs to them. It is a free gift of grace alone (see Eph. 2:8-9).

This is a process of growing in God that takes time and much prayer. How exciting it has been to me in my life of prayer to realize that, through prayer, we participate with God in what He desires to do in our lives today! This has helped me release the bondages of prejudice and criticism of others and any other barrier that hinders my relationships. Praying one for another enables the Holy Spirit to erase these things from our heart.

Grace-Filled Life

Through the years I have looked for praying people who have an intimate walk with Christ, because I have found I can learn much from them. Genuine sharing and learning takes place when we trust one another.

When Jim and I moved to Houston, I discovered that the lady who lived across the street from us, Mickie Winborn, was such a person. She was a beautiful Spirit-filled woman who shared her healing testimony with me.

In 1965, Mickie was riddled with cancer. The doctors had done everything medically possible, and the report that Mickie only had two weeks to live grieved her and her husband, Kenneth. Mickie wanted to stay alive and rear their two young sons. She remembered Marion Shockney's offer to fly with her to Pittsburgh for a Kathryn Kuhlman healing service. She asked Kenneth if she could fly to Pittsburgh with Marion to attend the meeting. She said to Kenneth, "What do I have to lose?" He agreed, and two days later Mickie and Marion were on a plane to Pittsburgh. They prayed much en route.

Without telling Mickie, Marion had contacted her friend David Wilkerson and told him she was bringing Mickie Winborn to a Kathryn Kuhlman healing service. David contacted Kathryn Kuhlman to share with her about Mickie's critical condition and positioned himself as an intercessor in Mickie's behalf. He said he would be in prayer that God, in His sovereignty, would extend His healing hand and touch her.

Mickie tells many wonderful stories of her two-and-one-half days in Pittsburgh. She says that even on death's door she was full of pride—not wanting anyone to know how sick she was, she put on her makeup and dressed immaculately. When they arrived at the church, much to her surprise, they were ushered to the front row. Mickie, a beautiful, gracious woman of God, was enjoying the service when Kathryn called her up for prayer. She could hardly believe she had been chosen. As Kathryn was praying for Mickie, she was delivered from a spirit of fear; fear of death, dying and being separated from her loved ones had plagued her. Instantly Mickie knew that God had set her free to complete her mission on Earth and that she would finish her days loving and serving God.

When Mickie returned to Houston, she chose to be at home with her family instead of returning to the hospital. Soon after, she had biopsies of the tumors on her breasts—no cancer was found! Fifteen months later, after much prayer and guidance from the Holy Spirit, she submitted to an exploratory operation. There still wasn't any cancer. Mickie had been healed!

God sovereignly touched and healed my friend, miraculously delivering her from cancer. She goes regularly to the doctor and has medical documentation for her healing. Through her own experience of this complete healing, God has lead her to a powerful ministry that has brought healing to many. She has ministered in services in Hong Kong, Panama, Costa Rica and extensively in the United States. In these meetings, tumors have fallen off; cancer has been healed; the handicapped have walked out of wheelchairs; backs and limbs have been healed; eyes have been opened; and all other manner of diseases have been cured.

Mickie has released an anointing in my own life to pray in divine faith for those needing healing. Although God had started this work in me back in New Jersey when He gloriously baptized me in His Holy Spirit, through Mickie Winborn's testimony there was a strengthening in my life to believe God. I now know the certainty, simplicity and love of Jesus Christ in a deeper way and believe it is the tender compassion of God that reaches out to us in our weakest moments, in our sickest moments and in our deepest despair. The compassion of love releases healing to us.

It is the cry of my heart that the compassion of Jesus will fill His church across the lands and the nations. I desire to see the day we will walk in the fullness of Christ, when we will see and feel His tender compassion. We shall be like Him as we are created in His image. At times, this marvelous love in its depth, richness and reality causes us to weep for hours with the compassionate heart of God. The love of God permeates, cleanses, heals and makes us whole.

He was wounded for our transgressions, He was bruised for our iniquities; the chastisement for our peace was upon Him; and by His stripes we are healed.

ISAIAH 53:5

CHAPTER 12

Mission Impossible? Not with God

If you have any doubt that prayer can change the course of history, let me tell you about my experiences with Russia. God wants us to pray boldly!

When I was a homemaker in Houston, Texas, in the 1970s, God impressed upon me to pray for the city of Moscow. "Did I hear You right, Lord?" I asked, since I then knew little about the Soviet Union or why God would put Russia on my prayer list. Nonetheless, I obeyed the Holy Spirit's leading, with no inkling that 17 years later I would travel to Russia to pray and minister in Jesus' name.

God tells us to ask Him to change the course of nations. "Ask of me, and I will make the nations your inheritance" (Ps. 2:8, *NIV*). I believe God mixed my humble prayers with millions of others uttered for the Russian people for many years. God is faithful—He keeps His promises. I have no doubt that the persistent, faithful prayers of many helped open the Iron Curtain, hastened the fall of communism and is bringing healing to Russia today.

Let me share memories of my visits to this nation.

Power of Prayer

In the shadow of Moscow's onion-shaped domes and sky-piercing spires, the young bride, dressed in her wedding gown, walked slowly across Red Square and approached the tomb of Lenin. As stone-faced guards looked on, she laid her bridal bouquet on the tomb and reserved a second bouquet to throw into the Lenin River. This was a state-required ritual symbolizing that the woman's marriage was first to the government of her country and second to her mate.

It was July 1990, and I was on my first prayer journey to Russia with six other women. We had felt that the Holy Spirit had spoken to us, telling us to go to Russia and to pray to open a path for the gospel. In preparation for the trip, we each read Jeremiah, dwelling particularly on these words: "Before you were born I sanctified you and appointed you as my spokesman to the world . . . you will go wherever I send you and speak whatever I tell you to. And don't be afraid . . . for I, the Lord, will be with you and see you through . . . I have put my words in your mouth!" (Jer. 1:5-9, *TLB)*.

The ministry of prayer was beginning to part the Iron Curtain, but Russia had not yet changed. It would be another year or more before it would be free of communist rule.

Daily we walked and prayed around Red Square, watching more Russian brides dutifully come and go. We decided to go to war in the spiritual realm, and we began to pray down strongholds and stand against the spiritual forces of evil that enslaved the people of this nation. For hours, we walked and quietly made prophetic declarations in God's name over what we saw: "Every one of those statues are going to come down. There will no longer be a marriage dedication to Lenin. Lord, we want to see those statues carried out on the shoulders of the people." Did I ever jump for joy, when almost two years later, on a television newscast, I saw Russians carry those statues out on their shoulders! It was powerful! It was God!

We as believers have the gift to bring forth life through the Holy Spirit.

We as believers have the gift to bring forth life. We felt God wanted us to labor and travail until the Holy Spirit hovered over this city and breathed His holy life upon the people of Moscow, drawing them to Jesus.

Every morning, my roommates and I arose at 5:00 A.M., went to the hotel window and read John 17 aloud over the city of Moscow. This chapter is Jesus' prayer and reveals His heart toward future believers. It also teaches us that the world is a battleground where the forces under Satan's power and those under God's authority are at war.

During the day, we walked different parts of the city, passing out gospel tracts and Bibles. People took these willingly, until one day, in one area, everybody refused them. We huddled together and commanded the spirit of darkness, who had blinded the spiritual eyes of these people to keep them from knowing God to be gone. I imagine you can guess what happened—everybody began to accept our tracts.

Another day, we rode with our two interpreters in a crowded train as we headed out of the city to visit an "underground" church. In the seat across from me sat a woman about my age. I tried to get her attention, but she would glance at me only for a moment and then look down. Still, this made an impression on me because in Russia, people keep their faces down in public—they do not look you in the eye. So I asked Steve, one of the interpreters, to ask her if I could give her a Bible.

As he spoke to her in Russian, tears flowed down her cheeks. She took the Bible I handed her and pressed it to her heart. When she opened it and discovered it was written in her language, she jumped up from her seat and kissed me first on one cheek, then the other, repeatedly.

"Bobbye," Steve explained to me in English, "she says she has been a Christian 37 years and has never had a Bible."

We got off the train at the next stop and then walked two miles before we came to the church in the woods. The church was actually an open-air, tentlike structure, and people stood because there were no chairs. The service had already begun so we joined in—and remained all six hours. Seven pastors spoke that day, and all of whom had been imprisoned for believing in Jesus—one pastor's eyes had been burned out. Their suffering pierced my heart.

At the altar call, 40 people received Christ as their Savior. The pastors decided to give the 40 Bibles we had brought to the newest converts, a sobering reminder that there is a world full of people God wants to bring to Himself.

The next day, we met with 10 Russian women and saw God literally transform them before our eyes. They were believers, but when God baptized them in His Holy Spirit, they jumped, sang and danced, praising Him. We invited them to join us that evening for dinner. When we arrived at the restaurant, I noticed one woman remained outside. When Steve and I went to check on her, we found her sobbing. Through tears, she explained, "I prayed many years ago to be allowed to go to a restaurant. God has answered my prayer." Steve and I wept with her.

Celebrating with these women enriched each of our lives. We felt led by the Spirit to return the next day and give them our clothing as a gift of God's love. God was using these small acts to teach us about blessing others. He wants us to love and care for one another even in simple ways, for whenever we show His love to others we are ministering to Him.

Extravagant Love

I'm reminded of the "love story" recorded in Luke 7:36-38. A woman, who was a sinner, came into Simon's home, where Jesus was an invited dinner guest, and washed Jesus' feet. What boldness! It was against the law for a Jewish woman to do such a thing. (I've wondered how she knew which man was Jesus.) Something was stirring within this woman, and she knew she had to get to Jesus. As she approached Him, she began to weep and her tears fell on His feet. She undid her hair, bent down and used her hair to dry His feet, and then she anointed His feet with expensive oil and tenderly kissed them.

Simon and the others in the room said, "If you only knew what kind of woman this was." Jesus *did* know, and He still loved her. He forgave her sins. He knows the lonely, hidden, hurting women in our midst, and He loves them. He wants extravagant love to reach them.

We are called as His Church to love with that kind of love. Ephesians 2:4-5 (*AMP*) tells us:

> But God–so rich is He in His mercy! Because of and in order to satisfy the great and wonderful and intense love with which He loved us, even when we were dead (slain) by [our own] shortcomings and trespasses, He made us alive together in fellowship and in union with Christ; [He gave us the very life of Christ Himself, the same new life with which He quickened Him, for] it is by grace (His favor and mercy which you did not deserve) that you are saved.

I go around saying, "grace, grace, grace." We need the grace of God for every moment of our lives. We cannot do the job alone. Unless the enabling grace fills us, we will fall flat on our faces. Grace to love, grace to work, grace to be a part of His calling, grace to strengthen you are all because of God's love. Sometimes we feel called—sometimes we don't. It is God's grace,

We need the grace of God every moment of our lives.

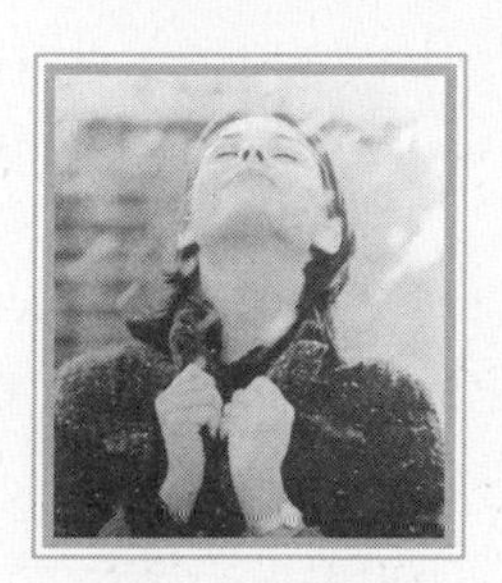

not our flesh, that allows each of us to walk in the call of God. We will turn one way and then another, but God says, "No, follow hard after Me. If I have called you to this, go with Me, because it is God you are following." Our acceptance by Him has nothing to do with our performance. It has to do with God's grace, God's anointing and God's holiness—His complete acceptance of us.

The Miracle Worker in Action

Four years later, in 1994, I returned to Russia. This time, I led an Aglow mission trip with 26 women who went to pray and minister.

One of our destinations was Nizhni Novgorod, a bumpy, 17-hour ride from Moscow. Here we were to meet Pastor Victor, who was also a medical doctor; he was to accompany our American group to minister in orphanages, prisons, hospitals and on city streets. When we stepped onto the train platform, gathering our mass of luggage, I heard someone calling, "Barbra, Barbra." I turned to see two men searching the crowd, and so I walked toward them.

"Are you the leader?" the younger man asked me in English. He was Eric, the translator.

"Yes, I am Barbara," I answered.

"May I present Victor, who is your pastor contact." Through the translator, Victor's first words to me were, "I do not believe in women ministers or women in leadership."

I caught my breath, praying how to respond lovingly to this unexpected declaration. "Victor," I said, "I am a woman and a leader, and I cannot change that. We have come to serve you."

Victor's displeasure was still evident as he accompanied us to an orphanage. We had brought toys, gifts and clothing for the children. Our women fell in love with these youngsters. Later, women from the team adopted two of them. I could sense Victor's attitude softening as he watched God's love in action through us.

The next day, some of our group did street ministry with mimes, songs and skits and then visited a hospital for terminally ill children. Victor and I took a team of 10 by bus to a women's prison. Our gifts of clothing, Bibles, books, makeup and medicines were left with the warden, who had told us not to mingle with the inmates—but we were not deterred. Guards led us to an auditorium where each of us gave a brief testimony about how the love of Christ had changed our lives.

There was much coughing going on in the room. I asked those who were ill to please stand up so that we could pray for them, and it seemed as if all 500 stood. God came in a very powerful way. The warden allowed me to give an altar call, and 300 women streamed forward to receive Christ as their Savior. The warden came to the stage and told the inmates our group would be allowed to mix and mingle with them. We hugged these women and spent the next two hours in personal ministry. The precious touch of God's love was present.

As we left, the warden asked if we would return the next day and minister to the children of the incarcerated women. "Yes," said Victor, "we'll bring all 26 women." On the bus, we saw another miracle. Victor knelt down and asked our forgiveness for his not recognizing women ministers.

What we saw the next day at the prison broke our hearts. The babies and toddlers of the women prisoners had no diapers—their tiny bodies were wrapped only in blankets. We hugged those precious little ones and prayed over each one for God's touch. As we left, many of the women came to us for parting hugs.

Before we left his city, Victor asked me to preach in his church on three occasions. The final evening, he knelt in front of all of us and his congregation and again asked forgiveness for his attitude. "Aglow" in Russian is translated as "radiant." He said, "These radiant women brought the Holy Spirit to Nizhni Novgorod."

The God of miracles wasn't finished with Nizhni Novgorod yet. At Victor's request, we visited a hospital for alcoholic women. The depressing building was a preview of what awaited us inside. We divided into teams and went to different rooms. In our room, we saw 10 bedridden women all hooked to intra venous feeding tubes. I had never been at such a loss for words as I was at that moment. Then, miraculously, the Holy Spirit seemed to fill this drab, distressing room with His presence. We knelt by each bed and prayed. Something was happening in these women's ravaged bodies.

A nurse came in to see what was going on. She checked each patient and started smiling. One by one, she removed their intravenous tubes, and, slowly, they all got out of bed. We formed a circle and began to sing "Amazing Grace." A few of them knew it and sang in their language as tears flowed freely. Then some asked Christ into their hearts. Before we left, all the patients gathered in a large room, where we celebrated God's healing touch on each life. Victor was crying—God's overcoming power had startled and amazed him.

On our last day in Nizhni Novgorod, Victor invited my team to see his medical clinic. He works full-time as a medical doctor as well as a pastor. Inside a large, old building, we walked up six flights of steps before we saw Victor's name on a door. It was his small home as well as a clinic. He had set up a table with six cups, a sliced banana and a few crackers. As Victor poured hot tea for us, his eyes beamed with appreciation. We knew he was sharing his best and blessing us with it.

Truly God used our prayers and our love to touch this Russian city. It was here, too, that God placed a burden in my heart to take the kind of street ministry we'd used in Russia to the cities of America. I had the privilege while I served as the U.S. national president of Aglow to set up short-term missions to 17 inner cities across our nation.

I have been to Russia prayer walking the streets three times, and today those who have come to Jesus Christ will now look you in the eye. You can tell who they are.

The Continuation of His Work

Today prayer is bringing more miracles to Russia. A newsletter has just arrived from Russia via e-mail from Alice Smith, executive director of the U.S. Prayer Center:

> Last night here in Kazakhstan (part of the old Soviet Union), I could hear from my room over 600 teens who were praising God at the top of their lungs. Realize that just 10 years ago, they lived in a society where they could

> not openly pray or serve God. Now, they are on fire for God in this nation—adults and kids. I wish you could experience their zeal and tears . . . I preach tomorrow in two services. This church has over 5,000 people in their congregation. The church growth in Kazakhstan is increasing 93 percent every year. Wow![1]

With God, nothing is impossible. Joy Dawson says, "He has shaped history around His people, and He expects us—not governments—to shape the history of the nations" (see 2 Chron. 7:14).

I believe the incredible global prayer thrust raised up this past decade is rallying God's armies of intercessors all over the world. When we pray effectively for a nation, God's hand is moved. May the prayers of God's people continue to be history shapers and history changers.

For as the soil makes the sprout come up and a garden causes seeds to grow, so the Sovereign LORD will make righteousness and praise spring up before all nations.

ISAIAH 61:11 (*NIV*)

CHAPTER 13

Check Your Vision

At the National Day of Prayer gathering in 1986, I was privileged to pray throughout the day in a small group with Cindy Jacobs. The speaker had asked us to pray with each other about our ministry, so I asked Cindy what she did. "My ministry is Generals of Intercession," she said. "We pray for the healing of nations."

I was fascinated. "How do you do that?" I asked.

"The same way you pray for the healing of a person," she replied.

I had never thought about an entire nation being healed. God was about to move my prayer-tent pegs much further out.

THE BEGINNING

Three years later, Jim and I were invited to attend the 1989 Lausanne II Congress in Manila. On the first morning, when I saw Cindy Jacobs, she invited us to have breakfast at her table and introduced us to Peter and Doris Wagner. After the breakfast, Dr. Wagner asked if I would serve as an intercessor in the 24-hour prayer room he had developed for the 11 days of the conference. Jim said he would like to serve in this capacity as well.

God's bottom line for intercession in that round-the-clock prayer room was to bring healing to the nations where sharing the gospel message was restricted or prohibited. Delegates from these nations poured into the prayer room seeking prayer for their individual nations. We learned that many of these had spent seven or more years in prison simply for believing in the name of Jesus, their homes and churches were raided and their families and friends were assaulted, tortured and murdered.

We wept openly for these pastors and for all they had suffered. I knew much about the Church throughout the world because of my long involvement with Aglow International, but I had never heard personal stories like these. Surely, God remembers every tear and identifies intimately with His persecuted Church. Now God was revealing their plight to us, their sisters and brothers in Christ and calling thousands of us to pray and stand with them in intercession as never before.

One morning at 4 A.M. a team of 8 to 10 were praying in the prayer room. We were covering the nations, when suddenly I heard God speaking to me, "I will begin a global prayer movement that will cover the face of the earth." At first I thought this message was in reference to the Aglow Network of Prayer. However, God began enlarging my vision that this was much larger than any one ministry. I was asked by another member of the group to share what I was sensing in my heart so I told them what I felt God was saying. This entire team, in unity, prayed that the Holy Spirit would bring this global prayer movement to fruition speedily.

Later a team of us met to discuss how the enemy of God had kept millions of people bound in darkness for so many decades. Cindy Jacobs shared a prophetic word she had earlier received from God: "Satan has an organized strategy to kill, steal and destroy, but My people have no counter plan, no strategy for defense." At this, we addressed the need for God's Church to understand spiritual warfare at a deeper level.

Peter Wagner took the lead and developed the Spiritual Warfare Network to bring together leaders who were involved in spiritual warfare around the world. Their goal was to learn from each other and hear from God.

Many Christian leaders have impacted my life deeply, and one of those people is Peter Wagner. His fervent, "red hot" love for God and His kingdom have greatly encouraged my call to intercession. At Lausanne II, I prayed 12 hours in the prayer room for the nations represented there, and then spent the next 12 hours praying specifically for Dr. Wagner. I did not sleep for 48 hours, so urgent was my call to do this. Only God knew what He was going to do, and I felt God was asking me to partner with Him to bring it forth. When I sense such strong heaviness and focus in my spirit, it's God's signal to me to pray for something important to His heart and His plans. "Here am I, Lord," I said.

I saw the holy call of God hovering over Dr. Wagner at the Lausanne Congress. God instructed me to pray for him, and for the following six months I prayed fervently for God's purposes and plans to unfold to Peter. In the holy quiet place with the Father, gathered in the embrace of the Son, I prayed with great grace, courage and boldness for Dr. Wagner. He became an apostle to the worldwide prayer movement that focused in the 1990s on global revival and completion of the Great Commission.

Intercession for spiritual leaders is the ministry of hidden prayer. Although there is a price to pay for such prayer, the privilege is always higher than the price.

During this time, Dr. Wagner asked me to be the prayer leader for the Spiritual Warfare Network he was convening. I asked Dutch Sheets to colead with me, and we gathered intercessors from across the nation to come to Colorado Springs at their own expense and spend the day praying while the Spiritual

Warfare Network met. This network of leaders met to learn from each other, to seek God's plans and strategies for bringing the lost to Him and, through intercessory prayer, to cooperate with Him to bring about His plans.

The intercessors prayed in a separate room. In an awesome day of prayer, led by the Holy Spirit, God gave us a strategy of Nehemiah and Ezra, the leader and the priest who were called to labor together. Our task was to complete the work of the kingdom of God by equipping the Church with weapons for spiritual warfare. The great harvest of souls was waiting.

The Church—that's us believers—will not fulfill its destiny until it truly becomes a house of prayer for all peoples.

This call pierced my heart. I saw a magnified need for prayer shields around our spiritual leaders across the United States and around the world for the warfare ahead. Our intercessory prayers can help shield them from harm and error.

Standing in support of Dr. Wagner, I was privileged over the next few years to invite teams of intercessors to travel to different nations and pray as he convened strategic meetings. These prayer rooms became "throne rooms" where we met God and His glory in ways I had never before imagined.

Intercession calls for us to deal with the unseen, including the unseen conflict or warfare being played out in the heavenlies between God and the evil one. This is the kingdom of light engaging the kingdom of darkness.

We were witnessing the development of a coordinated global prayer movement. Millions of people have been praying for years, in many places, and God was about to link those prayers in a new synergy. God was showing us that we were to be a unified force, empowering through prayer the whole Church to take the whole gospel to the whole world, and we soon realized this commission would require much deeper dependence on prayer.

My prayers for the nations continue to intensify with the heartbeat of God sounding within His people. He desires that all people be saved and none lost. He declared: "My house shall be called a house of prayer for all nations [*ethnos*]" (Isa. 56:7). All people, regardless of race, culture or language, need an opportunity to know about Christ. The Church—that's us believers—will not fulfill its destiny until it truly becomes a house of prayer for all ethnic peoples, for only through Him will all nations be truly unified and healed.

The ever-pursuing "hound of heaven" is seeking and opening new doors of opportunity. Nowadays, when we begin witnessing to someone, it seems that the ground already has been plowed and the seed sown for the person to receive Christ. We are seeing miraculous things in the worldwide Church.

Prayer is the fuel. God is mobilizing His people in united prayer to reach the unevangelized as never before. During the 1990s, there was intense prayer focused on behalf of the 65 nations located in the 10/40 Window (so named because of its latitude and longitude location on the globe). Thousands of intercessors were mobilized as many of us led or joined prayer teams traveling to these countries for on-site praying and still others prayed from their homes and churches. Now that the effort has expanded to the 40/70 Window to include countries in Europe, Scandinavia, north and central Asia.

God is raising up prayer warriors and visionaries who will seek Him for divine strategies to reach people in all nations. In

January 2000, Dr. Wagner said, "We are poised for the most massive prayer offensive into the kingdom of darkness that history has ever known." His prophetic words foretold of the great harvest to come.

I believe this word, because God promised it, and because I am seeing it come to fruition with my own eyes everywhere I turn these days. It is thrilling to witness more and more nations participate in prayer walking and prayer journeys. I myself have been honored to be a part of prayer journeys in Korea, China, Mongolia, Sri Lanka, Kuwait, Israel, Jordan, Greece, Turkey, Egypt, Cyprus and Russia. As I mingled with the people there, I heard many stories of miracles and supernatural breakthroughs in their nations.

Seeing God in a Fresh, New Way

I remember a vision God gave me three decades ago. As I prayed one morning at my Houston home, I saw a dark tunnel surrounded by hundreds of gardens filled with bright colored flowers, leafy trees and green grass. One by one, people emerged from the black tunnel; and as they stepped into this incredible garden, I saw Jesus opening His arms to welcome and embrace them. As they stepped from the dark place into the light and presence of Christ, they were immediately healed, delivered and freed from bondage. I was struck that it was a garden of abounding, transforming love. Through this vision, not only did God give me a peek at His global plan, but He also showed me that love is the key to transforming the earth. In order to reach the lost, His Church must operate under the canopy of God's love, righteousness and justice that overarches all the nations.

At that time, I did not know what this vision meant. However, it gave me hope that all people in darkness could be miraculously transformed in His love and that I was to pray for this to happen.

Prophetic visions and prophetic words show us what is in God's heart. But we must be patient, for God will only bring them to pass in His timing.

I believe with all my heart that God wants His power manifested through His Church as never before. He wants the captives freed from years of darkness and bondage, but He wants to release to us more than just His power. He wants to show us the full expression of Jesus Christ our Lord and Savior, the Holy One to whom every knee ultimately will bow. He wants to move us closer to the throne room of heaven. He wants our churches to be places of worship where He is welcome to come, to walk in our midst, to sit with us and stir in us those deep things He already has sown. He wants to inhabit His house, not just visit it.

I have walked with the Lord for almost four decades, and I am beginning to see God in a fresh, new way. I am thrilled with the visitations and revelations He is giving to His Church, but I long for His habitation. I have a passionate zeal to see the Father's house become all He desires it to be, so He will come and fill it with His Holy presence.

I agree with God Chaser Tommy Tenney that "the coming revival is not about sermons and information; it's going to be about worship and impartation." He's talking about the same manifest presence that transformed Saul of Tarsus "from a persecutor into a propagator of the gospel. Now picture the glory of God riveting entire communities with conviction after engulfing them in the light of His glory." [1]

Prayer and worship bring God's presence. From His presence, Damascus Road experiences will come to Earth in "suddenly" swoops as they did on the Day of Pentecost. Imagine us with praying, worshiping arms propping open the windows of heaven so the transforming glory of God would fall in the streets of every city in every nation. This is my fervent prayer.

How big is your miracle vision? According to Joy Dawson, if your vision is not world vision, it's too small. The Bible has hundreds of references to spreading the Word of God to the nations. If it's God's priority, it should be ours, too. Ask God to stretch your vision.

How precious is Your lovingkindness, O God! Therefore the children of men put their trust under the shadow of Your wings. They are abundantly satisfied with the fullness of Your house, and You give them drink from the river of Your pleasures. For with You is the fountain of life; in Your light we see light.

PSALM 36:7-9

CHAPTER 14

South Korea—Land of Prayer

The humility and reverence of the Christians in South Korea have always attracted me. I had studied about the South Korea Prayer Movement in the 1960s long before I visited that land. The growth of the Korean Churches was explosive during the 1970s and 1980s, and I remember being intrigued that a Buddhist nation was turning to Christianity. The Koreans I have met attribute this conversion to fervent prayer that was launched in that land. As a result, many people were responding to the gospel and their lives were being changed.

I've been honored to be in Korea four times, and I have come to love the people and land deeply. They are a very friendly and generous people who have such a gift of hospitality. It is evident to me that God has touched them for His holy purposes, and I believe the Western Church has much to learn from them.

HIS LOVE AGLOW IN KOREA

The Aglow Prayer Council, which had led the movement of prayer in the United States, planned an Aglow prayer journey to Korea. Twenty-six women answered the call, and in 1992 this trip became a reality. As God was breathing His life for prayer deeply into Aglow, He was also breathing prayer upon His ministry to women around the world. So this trip was special for all of us.

Several of our council members had been asked to speak at the Korean National Conference, where we experienced a wonderful time of worship and prayer. Each session was packed with the holy presence and power of God as each speaker shared the things God had put on her heart. It was a time of our team bonding with the Korean women, and it didn't take long for us to fall in love with them.

After the conference, we began walking through Seoul praying warfare prayers over the city out of our desire to dislodge some ancient strongholds. We linked our prayers with the prayers the Koreans had been praying for years, and we felt the power of God in our midst.

We traveled by bus around the nation, stopping occasionally to pray. One of our strategies was to pray at the demarcation line which separates South and North Korea. Standing on it you see what is called the Bridge of No Return. We sensed God leading us to pray that the name would be changed to the Bridge of Reunification. I know all of us rejoiced when the North Koreans did cross that bridge years later and were reunited to their families. Yet even though some of the restrictions have been relaxed, a hostile situation still exists.

Another point of interest to us was visiting Prayer Mountain, which many describe as "open heaven praying." There I was struck by the sincerity of the Koreans in their pursuit of God–I saw that prayer was a way of life for them. The spiritual inheritance of the Koreans reminds me of Jacob's journey of faith.

Genesis 28 tells the story of Jacob leaving home and coming to a certain place. He took a stone, placed it under his head and fell asleep. He began to dream and saw a ladder was set up on the earth, and its top reached to heaven; and there the angels of God were ascending and descending it. "The LORD stood above it and said, 'I am the LORD God of Abraham your father and the God of Isaac; the land on which you lie I will give to you and your descendants.' Then Jacob awoke from his sleep and said, 'Surely the LORD is in this place, and I did not know it.' . . . 'This is none other than the house of God, and this is the gate of heaven'" (Gen. 28:13,16-17).

Jacob, when he lay his head upon the rock, was laying on the covenant promises of God, the very spot where His father Abraham had built an altar to God. I call this praying under an open heaven.

We visited Prayer Mountain in Korea with one of our hosts, Dr. David Cho. Once we reached Prayer Mountain, we were led to a small auditorium where we could have a time of prayer, sharing and edifying teaching. Being in this place of continual prayer 24 hours a day was an inspiration to each of us and reminded me of one of my favorite Scriptures, Isaiah 56:6-7:

> Also the sons of the foreigner who join themselves to the LORD, to serve Him, and to love the name of the LORD, to be His servants—everyone who keeps from defiling the Sabbath, and holds fast My covenant—even those I will bring to My holy mountain, and make them joyful in My house of prayer. Their burnt offerings and their sacrifices will be accepted on My altar; for My house shall be called a house of prayer for all nations.

Due to the heavy rain we had to make a decision whether to leave or stay. We were told that if any stayed, we would be picked up the next morning. Despite the rains, 10 of us decided to spend the night. Although there was a hotel facility available, I wanted to stay in one of the prayer huts, since I had dreamed of this for ages. My spirit was deeply moved by what I felt in this place.

At the end of my all-night prayer vigil, the dawn broke forth in radiant splendor. The rain had ceased, but the water glistened on the grass. The words of one of my favorite songs, "In the Garden," stirred in my soul. I walked alone through a garden singing:

I come to the garden alone,
While the dew is still on the roses;
And the voice I hear,
Falling on my ear,
The Son of God discloses.

He speaks and the sound of His voice
Is so sweet the birds hush their singing;
And the melody
That He gave to me
Within my heart is ringing.

I'd stay in the garden with Him
Tho the night around me be falling;
But He bids me go
Thru the voice of woe,
His voice to me is calling.

And He walks with me,
And He talks with me,
And He tells me I am His own;
And the joy we share
As we tarry there
None other has ever known.[1]

I met up with the others as we walked up the steep hill to a place overlooking the mountains of North Korea. We stretched our arms toward it and prayed for healing between North and South Korea. Tears flowed as God revealed to us His intense love for the masses who do not know Him in Korea as well as other nations. God's heart is always to bring His redemptive love to the individual as well as the multitudes.

On our bus ride home, we were all sharing our experiences. Each one was glad she had made the decision to stay. Those in the hotel had a chance to share and pray together. I looked at two of my Aglow companions, Sue Parmenter and Judy Ball.

God's heart is always to bring His redemptive love to the individual as well as the multitudes.

The sight of us made me start laughing–we looked like bedraggled, drenched cats. We had been scheduled to meet three pastors when we returned to the hotel. They were to escort us to lunch and then to the Korean School of Evangelism, where I'd been invited to speak. They were waiting for us at the hotel, but I asked them to wait while we hurriedly freshened up. One look at us and they understood why! The lunch was delightful–we sat on the floor and ate Korean style. The conversation flowed freely, and the pastors acquainted us with Korean customs.

Korea's Missionaries

Later that same day I addressed approximately 500 graduates who were going into mission work. This gift from God was an extreme privilege; I was told it was the first time an American woman had spoken at this school. After I finished speaking, Judy, Sue and I anointed each graduate with oil and imparted an empowering to go forth from Korea to the mission fields of the world. We knew they would take the love of Jesus and the glorious prayer movement God had started in Korea to the nations of the world.

The important role that Korea would play in fulfilling the Great Commission became even more evident to me in 1993 when Dr. Peter Wagner asked me to take a team of intercessors to the Gideon's Army meeting in Korea in October. I had served as Dr. Wagner's prayer leader since 1990. My horizon for prayer was expanding. The intercessors had spent many hours in intercessory prayer in preparation for this global gathering, and we had prayed for two years over names listed on a piece of paper. Now, we were meeting the leaders and putting faces with the names that we had held before God in prayer.

Our prayer room was open 24 hours a day. Our assignment as intercessors was to pray for the entire gathering, seek the face of God and allow Him to pray prayers through us. We had six teams, and each team served two three-hour prayer sessions, one during the day and one at night. I had appointed a team captain and cocaptain for each team before we got to Korea, which helped keep things on track. I had key intercessors who knew how to intimately engage the Holy Spirit and see God move in our midst. We all met together every morning at 6:00 A.M. and then again each evening at 6:00 P.M. to pray and debrief.

As we came together in intercession, one word describes the experience, *"awesome."* His presence filled the room, hour after hour. The Holy Spirit led each of our teams, on one particular day, independently, to pray specifically for the children of the world. The Holy Spirit is the best leader of prayer because we can trust Him fully. Always in the prayer room we find the combination of worship and prayer are married and can't be separated.

The Holy Spirit hovered over us, creating a holy atmosphere as we bowed before Him praying on behalf of all nations for harvest.

After the sessions closed each evening, our prayer room filled with delegates from around the world. The intensity of prayer was almost more than our physical bodies could endure, but this team of intercessors persevered along with the delegates and brought forth the heart of God for the nations.

On the closing night Peter asked me to give a report to the Gideon's Army delegates on the happenings in the prayer room. It was a holy moment for me as intercessors shared some of the deep holy experiences that had been going on in the prayer room. Most of them had prayed with us, so they were already acquainted with the Spirit's activity.

Since Peter Wagner has always honored intercessors and made them a vital part of his ministry, he gave me permission to anoint each delegate with oil after they received Communion. Assisted by my friend and brother in the Lord, Wesley Tullis, we anointed with oil and laid hands on each delegate. We prayed for the House of Prayer to be established in each individual and nation. Both of us have carried this passion in our heart for years.

AD2000 Consultation

Two years later I returned to Korea as part of the United Prayer Track. Dr. Wagner asked Ben Jennings and Chuck Pierce to assist me in leading prayer for the AD2000 Consultation. He asked us to recruit 120 intercessors for this great event. Peter wanted us to have an Upper-Room experience like the one on Pentecost. Fifty-two intercessors from America, 14 from other nations and 60 from Korea prayed around the clock.

Our intercession was to bring forth the heart of God for the

AD2000 Consultation. We were now working under the leadership of Luis Bush and Thomas Wang, who were the leaders for the entire consultation, and throughout our 10 days together I stayed in close touch with Luis Bush.

The focus of the gathering was global evangelism. There were plenary sessions each morning and evening, but afternoons allowed a variety of interest groups called tracks. Delegates who visited the prayer room shared how God's spirit was moving across their nation in astonishing ways. I was reminded of the words of the prophet in Habakkuk 1:5: "Look among the nations and watch–be utterly astounded! For I will work a work in your days which you would not believe, though it were told you."

Here in Korea, I saw anew how many different ministries around the globe were partnering to see the entire world evangelized and the Great Commission fulfilled. And I, an ordinary woman from the faraway plains of Texas, was in the middle of it.

Reconciling the Nations to Each Other–and to Himself

It was during this gathering that I was struck by the reality that intercessors are history shapers and future shapers. The two come together in God. Intercessors hear from God in a different way as they grow intimately connected to Him. Holy intimacy is the secret of an Upper-Room experience–this relationship shows us God's heart as He reveals His plans for the future of every nation: reconciliation and fullness of life.

The revelation began on the fourth day of the Consultation, when 65 intercessors gathered in the prayer room seeking instruction from the Lord. I read from the book of Revelation 4:1: "After these things I looked, and behold, a door standing open in heaven. And the first voice which I heard was like a trumpet speaking with me, saying, 'Come up here, and I will show you things which must take place after this.'"

I continued reading from chapter 4 and then began to read chapter 5. When I read the eighth verse, the glory of the Lord filled the prayer room. I was consumed by the burning fire of God and fell on my face. My Bible flew out of my hand as I fell to the floor, and I was immobilized by the presence of a Holy God. Occasionally I would hear groans as His Holy Fire consumed additional intercessors. One woman who knew me well wanted to walk over to see if I was all right. As she started toward me, the fear of God gripped her, and she screamed, fearing she would die on the spot. She saw the presence of the glory of God and fell on her face weeping. The fullness of God came upon many, clothing them in His presence. Suddenly, like a mighty rushing wind, the intercessors fell on their faces worshiping the holiness of God. For three hours we had an Upper Room experience. The Holy Spirit ministered to us individually and corporately. During that holy time with His presence filling the room, we were touched, changed and challenged to walk humbly before our God.

The next day we prayed in the prayer room for 15 hours without stopping. Most of us never sat. God had shown us this was a time to stand in warfare for the nations, as key leaders from the consultation were in the prayer room and joined in fervent prayer. Reconciliation began to unfold with the Koreans and the Japanese. Then representatives of the nations surrounding Israel gathered in the prayer room to pray for Israel. At this point delegates from Israel walked into the prayer room. The Israeli delegates were deeply moved as they heard the prayers being prayed for their nation. The delegates from the nations that surround Israel gathered around Israeli delegates to ask forgiveness of her from their nations. As they continued in prayer, Jews and Arabs were reconciled.

A domino effect began with Turkey asking forgiveness from

the Armenians, and delegates from Iraq asking forgiveness from Kuwaiti delegates for invading their land. Suddenly all the delegates from many of the Middle East nations were sobbing and lovingly embracing each other. One of the leaders from Iran began to speak. He was anointed for this moment. Once again, we were all on our faces before God asking forgiveness for the sins of our nations. We knew many of these delegates would pay a price for their bravery.

Reconciliation is on God's heart for all people groups, genders, generations and denominations. He wanted to release His power to heal all nations through the intercessors. And He chose to make a start that day in Korea. What a beautiful testimony to the perseverance of the believers there!

The Continuing Mission of the Korean Believers

I returned to Korea in 1998 to speak at the Korean National Aglow Conference. A dear friend, Judy Ball, accompanied me. We were treated with grace and love throughout the conference—their hospitality made us feel so much at home. Judy and I stayed up long hours at night ministering His love to these beautiful women who were so sensitive to the Holy Spirit. During the closing night about 2,000 people from Youth With A Mission joined us. Again, we witnessed the fullness God is developing in Korea as they reverently prayed, worshiped and honored Christ in simple ways. It was a power-packed closing and one we will long remember as God moved so mightily in our midst. To Him belongs all praise, honor and glory!

Where I now live, in Colorado Springs, we have 12 Korean churches. I've been privileged to preach in two of them and to meet and know beautiful Korean men and women in my city. Two precious Korean ladies, Kay and Angie, who work in the beauty salon I frequent, both have blessed my life immensely. A deep bond of love has developed as we share our joys and sorrows as sisters in the Lord and pray for one another.

I have been honored to walk among these people who demonstrate reverence, friendliness, courtesy, honor and love. It is evident they have been touched by God for His purposes.

He is the image of the invisible God, the firstborn over all creation. For by Him all things were created that are in heaven and that are on earth, visible and invisible, whether thrones or dominions or principalities or powers. All things were created through Him and for Him. And He is before all things, and in Him all things consist. And He is the head of the body, the church, who is the beginning, the firstborn from the dead, that in all things He may have the preeminence.

COLOSSIANS 1:15-18

CHAPTER 15

God's Heart in Action

In late summer 1999, eyes and hearts around the world turned toward the nation of Turkey. On August 17, an earthquake registering 7.4 on the Richter scale struck the heavily populated western region of this ancient country. The quake and its relentless aftershocks devastated the land and created emotional havoc in the hearts of the Turkish people. Some 20,000 died, buried under the rubble of collapsed buildings; more than 42,000 were injured, and at least 60,000 were left without homes.

Survivors grappled with shortages of water, food and fuel, fires and the looming threat of disease. Rescue efforts, witnessed by television viewers around the world, were hampered by steady rain and cold weather.

Gripped by the news accounts of the tragedy, my husband, Jim, and I were praying about it from our Colorado home a day later.

"Father God," I prayed, "I ask You to send people who would be tender, compassionate and loving to minister Your love amid this devastation."

Then, I sensed God saying, "You go, Bobbye."

As I was sharing this with Jim, the telephone

rang. It was a call inviting me to serve on the International Health Services and Disaster Relief team being dispatched immediately to Turkey. Jim said, "Yes, go."

Within 24 hours I joined other Americans on a Christian relief team led by Drs. Betsy and Mark Neuenschwander, medical doctors who are also ordained ministers and teachers. We arrived in Turkey, lugging 18 suitcases of medicines. I had never seen anything like what I saw then—the devastation cannot be comprehended by looking at television pictures. Huge buildings in three cities were leveled. Two city blocks, including a large hotel with its doomed guests, literally fell into the sea. A whole campsite where 300 children were sleeping slipped into the sea. The streets and temporary tents teemed with injured and traumatized men and women, and dazed, orphaned children played in mounds of debris. Unrelenting rain filled the tents and soaked mattresses, cots, everything. People wept constantly.

"God's face is toward those who suffer," says Dr. Betsy Neuenschwander. When intercessors keep asking God to share with them the concerns closest to His heart, they will inevitably be turned to the world's hurting children and cast-off people.

I was privileged to be there as a crisis intercessor and trauma counselor, and I trusted the Holy Spirit would lead us, minute by minute, to do what we'd come to do—show forth His love and His hope.

From sunrise to dark I talked, wept and prayed with grieving people, always asking their permission. Since Turkey is an Islamic nation, one has to receive permission to pray in Isa's (Jesus') name.

God moved in miraculous ways.

Praying in the Name of Jesus

One woman lost 16 members of her family. Her five-year-old granddaughter was all she had left. I was summoned to a tent where the child lay nearly lifeless with a raging fever.

I silently pleaded with God, "Don't let this grandmother's last relative die. Bring her back to life."

The Holy Spirit reminded me of how Elijah prayed to raise a widow's son in the story recorded in 1 Kings 17:19-22. He picked up the child and stretched his body over him, praying, "Let this child's soul come back to him."

I told the translator, "I'm going to pray in the faith of Elijah." I lifted the limp girl and held her to my chest, spreading my body over hers. As I prayed, I began to feel a shaking in the child's body—God was restoring her to life.

This was a beautiful gift of God's love to the grieving grandmother, reminding me that His miracles are expressions of His compassion to the suffering. They also demonstrate the supernatural power of Jesus Christ to Muslims, Hindus and other non-Christians who need the evidence of miracles before they embrace the God-man, Jesus Christ, and believe.

The news of the restored child and the power of the name of Isa (Jesus) spread and soon others wanted to know Him. The next day I received an invitation to meet with 10 Muslim women, each telling of her almost unbearable personal crisis. We wept with them, anointed each with oil and prayed that they would come to know the Christ who would bring supernatural healing into their lives.

Day after day, sick and injured people lined up for blocks to be treated by our medical team. One day, my attention was drawn to a man who was impatient and irritated by the long wait. I approached him; his companion told me the man was blind and needed medical care.

"Do you know that Isa, the Prophet and healer of Islam, healed the blind?" I asked them both. "May I pray for you in the name of Isa?"

When both agreed, I laid my hands upon the blind man's eyes and quietly asked Isa to heal them. Suddenly, to my thrill and shock, the man announced he could see. The two of them left joyfully.

My heart overflowed with praise, but I said nothing. We were cautioned to be quiet when we prayed, in order to avoid arousing the suspicion or ire of the Muslim guards.

We must demonstrate the love and compassion of Christ, not just speak about it.

Sometimes, God's healings were solely spiritual and released through simple actions to communicate God's unfathomable compassion to someone's spirit. One morning, Betsy Neuenschwander summoned me to the medical tent where she was attending a woman with severe psoriasis, a skin ailment.

"We have no medicine to treat this," Betsy told me. "Will you pray with her?"

Sometimes, we must demonstrate the love and compassion of Christ, not just speak about it. The more time we spend in prayer with Him, the deeper our longings to know and understand the Father's heart and the more effective intercessors we will be.

"What would *You* do here, Father?" I prayed silently. I led the woman to the trauma tent, where Susan, a fellow intercessor, and I, simply cradled her in our embrace and poured soothing oil over her dry, scarred arms.

She began to weep. "It has been 15 years since anyone has touched me," she sobbed.

As God opened her heart, we then told her about Isa and His deep love for the lepers. When she left, she was smiling.

My intercessor friend Joy Dawson, says, "God's purpose is not to make us sad when we see the hurting people of the world, but to help us to become more like Him through entering into 'the fellowship of sharing in His sufferings'" (see Phil. 3:10).

Supernatural Revelation

One of the most miraculous stories I witnessed in Turkey involves a beautiful 15-year-old Turkish girl who came to our trauma tent. Her name was Rayfa. She had started having dreams and visions when she was 13, and her Muslim parents thought she had lost her mind.

As she described her dreams to me, I sensed a destiny of God upon this young woman's life. She said she had seen a man dressed in white, standing a long distance from her. He appeared night after night for weeks, then disappeared for about six months. When the dream returned recently, this time, the man dressed in white was close enough that she could see he had a belt of gold and a sword at his side. As the dreams progressed, she saw him riding on a white horse, coming down steps toward her. He was reaching out to her, but she could not reach him over a chasm that separated them. The dreams stopped, and she did not see him again for a season.

Christians may recognize this image from the book of Revelation 19:11: "Now I saw heaven opened, and behold, a white horse. And He who sat on him was called Faithful and True, and in righteousness He judges and makes war." But this was a Muslim girl who had never seen a Bible nor heard the story or name of Jesus Christ.

I met with Rayfa several times to hear her stories, and I could see that God had chosen to reveal Himself to this Kurdish woman. We are hearing reports from around the world of Muslims and other unevangelized people having miraculous revelations of Jesus Christ as the Son of God and conversions following them. There are no evangelists, no crusades or books, only the supernatural, sovereign revelation of God.

The next time I saw Rayfa, she told me that five days before the earthquake, the man in white had appeared to her again and told her to warn her family and friends to sleep outside on August 17, because there would be a dreadful earthquake in Turkey. She persuaded her whole family to do it. "I have to obey the man in white," she told them.

The house her family lived in was demolished that night, but they were not harmed. A 16-story apartment complex next to their house was crushed, and friends who had failed to heed Rayfa's warning died in the quake. The next time she saw the man in white in a dream, he was so close she almost could reach him.

The more I heard, the more I realized God was revealing Himself to her in a unique and mighty way. Perhaps Rayfa is God's Esther for Turkey.

I was mindful that it is against the law to minister to a minor in Turkey, so I had sent a letter to her parents asking if I could share with her about the God who created the heavens and the earth. They agreed. I told her, "If the man in white appears to you again, inquire of him, 'What is your name?'" If she knew through revelation who the man in white was, I would be free to risk sharing with her.

Three days later when I returned to the camp where Rayfa was, she skipped over to me and announced, "Bobbye, His name is Isa."

Susan and I offered her a Bible, but she was reluctant to take it, fearing it "might cause trouble in my home." Then to our amazement, she declared, "Isa, the man in white, lives in my heart."

The night we said good-bye, she said, "Bobbye, I would love to visit you in the United States, but if I do not see you again on this earth, I will be with you in heaven."

I wept. This young woman had not received any special training or study, and she lives in an Islamic nation, yet she knew we would be together in heaven. God is revealing Himself in miraculous ways around the globe today.

I believe that in my lifetime I will know, in some way, that God is using Rayfa in a miraculous way. Until then, I will hold her before God's throne in intercession.

Even in crises, the Lord's calling is not to a work, but to Himself. I believe prayer is the greatest work on Earth, and I saw it fulfilled amidst the devastation in Turkey and in the lives of those who had lost so much. Wherever we go, if we live out of His presence, we will see lives transformed and healed.

Is anyone among you suffering? Let him pray. Is anyone cheerful? Let him sing psalms. Is anyone among you sick? Let him call for the elders of the church, and let them pray over him, anointing him with oil in the name of the Lord. And the prayer of faith will save the sick, and the Lord will raise him up. And if he has committed sins, he will be forgiven. Confess your trespasses to one another, and pray for one another, that you may be healed. The effective, fervent prayer of a righteous man avails much. Elijah was a man with a nature like ours, and he prayed earnestly that it would not rain; and it did not rain on the land for three years and six months. And he prayed again, and the heaven gave rain, and the earth produced its fruit.

JAMES 5:13-18

CHAPTER 16

Kettle and Bowl—The Miraculous in America

I stared up at the towers of Northampton, Massachusetts. I could almost hear the prayers of Jonathan Edwards, David Brainerd and other godly Americans of the past echoing in this place. *The land beneath my feet*, I thought, *is saturated with prayers of generations past, and we have come in this summer of 2001 to add our prayers to those uttered before we were born*. We had come to the New England states to "redig the wells" of revival in the United States and to reclaim our godly historical inheritance. We had come to pray for a supernatural breakthrough in the heavenlies that would hasten God's healing and restoration of our country.

Walking and kneeling, we bathed this Massachusetts land again in prayer to God Almighty. Our voices blended and rose to a crescendo. So intense were the prayers, that "suddenly" I felt the ground beneath my sandaled feet actually tremble. It was slight, but

I could tell from the astonished looks on the people near me that I had not imagined it.

Ah, those "suddenlies" of God. I love this phrase, "the days of God's suddenlies," coined by Jack Hayford, pastor of The Church On The Way in Van Nuys, California. It so aptly summarizes the outpouring of God's spirit we are witnessing around the world in the dawn of this new millennium.

Prayer and intercession–globally coordinated–are lighting the fuse to release the explosive power of the Holy Spirit. Revival is suddenly on the lips of Christian believers everywhere, and nations long closed to the gospel are being opened. People of all races, ethnicities and religions are coming to Christ in the most awesome, thrilling movement I have witnessed in my six decades of living.

Dutch Sheets calls this phenomenon God's ordained synergy of the ages. God gave Dutch this term in 1999 and revealed to him that this synergy is about to happen in God's eternal clock. Simply defined, synergy occurs when people (or forces) working together achieve a multiplied result, or force, they are incapable of achieving alone or separately.

I agree with Dutch that God's people are about to achieve breakthroughs in the heavenlies that will change things on earth that we've been unable to change with human will and wisdom alone.

Prayer Kettle

Northampton, Massachusetts, was one stop on the second leg of a prayer journey named the "Kettle Tour" that covered nine cities and eight universities. Dutch Sheets, Will Ford and Lou Engle led this remarkable prayer blitz. I traveled with a team of 30 intercessors and a large, 250-year-old cooking kettle once used by American slaves.

This kettle, used for praying as well as cooking and washing clothes, passed down through the generations of Will Ford's family. The slaves, as Will Ford tells it, were owned by a cruel master who prohibited praying, since he thought they were praying for their freedom. In order to keep their prayers from being heard, these slaves would gather in a barn late at night. They would turn the kettle upside down, place it up on rocks to elevate it and then get down and pray underneath it so that the kettle absorbed the sound of their prayers. It turns out that the slaves weren't praying for their own freedom at all, but for their children and future generations.

The "prayer kettle" belongs to a young African-American, William (Will) Ford III and his wife, Michelle. It had been handed down through generations from Will's slave ancestors.

So how did it end up on a revival tour?

In March of 2001, Will attended the prayer conference in Colorado Springs hosted by Dutch Sheets. Will heard Dutch Sheets share a teaching that we not only can pray in agreement with the person sitting next to us, but we can also agree with the prayers of past generations. He stated that these prayers are still alive today before the throne of God and that our agreeing in prayer with them would produce a synergy of the ages.

Will thought of the kettle his family owned and wept when he realized that he could join his prayers with those of his ancestors for his and future generations. Through much prayer, Will and Michelle agreed to bring the kettle and accompany Dutch and Billy to Williamsburg. It was then decided by Dutch and Lou Engel that the kettle should be taken throughout the Northeast and New England with a team of intercessors.

Dutch said God had revealed that our prayer plan should picture three things: (1) the synergy released through joining of races, generations and prayer of agreement; (2) the redigging of wells of revival, with the kettle representing past generations;

and (3) the bowls mentioned in Revelation 5:8; 8:3-5 and Zechariah 14:20, filled with the prayers of God's people, mixed with the fire of God and then poured upon the earth.

"We have prayed fervently and a long time for the healing and unity between American generations, races, genders and denominations," Dutch explained. "And we must continue to pray for increasing interracial and intergenerational cooperation, which will result in synergistic power of unprecedented proportions. God has brought about opportune times in our nation where tremendous reconciliation and healing has occurred."[1]

On the Kettle Tour, Dutch instructed us that we, filled with faith, were praying for a supernatural breakthrough in the heavenlies. We were to add our prayers to all the prayers that had been previously prayed in these regions. We were not doing this because the local people needed us; rather, we had been sent by a mandate from God to pray openly for revival, restoration and the healing of our land to see our nation turn back to God. Acts 3:19 tells us, "Repent therefore and be converted, that your sins may be blotted out, so that times of refreshing may come from the presence of the Lord."

Williamsburg, Virginia

What a historic and holy time it was! July 26th we flew to Washington, D.C. Then 30 people divided into four vans, and we drove to Williamsburg, Virginia, for the first part of our Kettle Tour. We were hosted by New Life Christian Center, and the people there were wonderful to us. I will share briefly about the first leg of the Kettle Tour.

In Jamestown, we prayed at the site of the first church in America and then walked to the James River. I loved the symbolic healing ceremony that took place there. Derek Brant, a dear brother, from London, England, joined us to serve as a "father" from England coming to bless the sons and daughters of America. Derek had waded into the Thames River in London before he left and fetched a rock from the river where the first ships departed for America hundreds of years ago. Now, in July 2001, Derek waded into the James River at the site where those ships had docked in America; then he turned and walked out of the river up an embankment carrying the rock on an open Bible. This time, the Native Americans on our team made a human "gate of entry" to welcome him to this land. Derek, representing England, presented the rock to Dutch and prayed a "father's" blessing over all the sons and daughters in America. After a time of strategic, powerful praying for breakthrough and turning in our nation, suddenly waves began to wash up on the shore; yet there was no wind, nor had there been any previous waves. Powerful! Many of us were moved to tears at this touching moment.

We drove to the Gospel Spreading Farm, the location to which slaves were first taken when they entered the country in 1619. They were housed in a barn on the level under the area where the working mules were kept. The site is now a Christian camp. We had a great time of prayer there and spoke biblical declarations over the land.

Our next stop was Williamsburg, Virginia, where, together with local pastors and leaders, we had a powerful, prophetic time of prayer and intercession. We went to the Middle Plantation, the original site of Williamsburg, where a seven-mile-long wall was built in 1622 to divide the races. This was such an overwhelmingly spiritual stronghold that at first the leadership was not certain we were supposed to deal with it. Yet, after an intense time of travail and seeking the Lord's wisdom, God revealed His strategy—humility. The site represented the location where the spirits of isolation, segregation, separation and racism entered our nation. Those strongholds were powerful, but God led us step by step as we pierced the darkness with His select warfare arrows. It was a time of great humility as Will, Jim and Dutch washed each other's feet in the kettle, symbolically representing three nations: the Native Americans, the Africans and "the white men," as the natives called them.

In that moment, Matthew 16 seemed to come alive before my eyes.

> [Jesus asked] "Who do men say that I . . . am?" Simon Peter answered and said, "You are the Christ, the Son of the living God." Jesus answered and said to him, "Blessed are you, Simon Bar-Jonah, for flesh and blood has not revealed this to you, but My Father who is in heaven. And I also say to you that you are Peter, and on this rock I will build My church, and the gates of Hades shall not prevail against it. And I will give you the keys of the kingdom of heaven, and whatever you bind on earth will be bound in heaven, and whatever you loose on earth will be loosed in heaven" (vv. 16:13,16-19).

We had moved in the humility, authority and power of the God who sent us. I then knew that the gates of hell would not prevail against His Church.

GETTYSBURG

We had an incredible time praying and declaring the Word of God when we gathered around the kettle on the Gettysburg battleground. We battled against a deep spirit of grief. Isaiah 46:8-11 tells us we are to remember the things of old–all the transgressions–hearing God say to us, "I am God, and there is no other; I am God, and there is none like Me. Declaring the end from the beginning, and from ancient times things that are not yet done. . . 'My counsel shall stand, and I will do all My pleasure,' calling a bird of prey from the east, the man who executes My counsel, from a far country." We kept our eyes fixed on Jesus, who never lost sight of where he was headed—that exhilarating

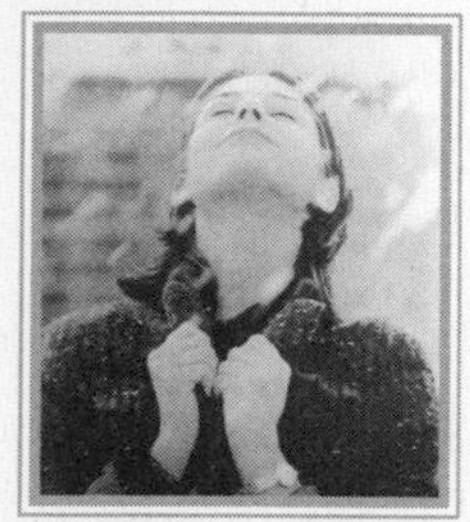

We must keep our eyes on Jesus, who never lost sight of where He was headed—that exhilarating finish with and in God.

finish with and in God (see Heb. 12:2-3). We came from Colorado and other states to the East Coast. Like a hawk, who represents the apostolic anointing to bring things back to right order and alignment, we swooped down upon the land held so long by the enemy of God. I sensed God saying to me, "I have purposed these Kettle Tours. Indeed, I have spoken it and I have brought them to pass. My salvation shall not linger. I will place salvation in Israel and America." We are linked together, intertwined, bound together in God.

WASHINGTON, D.C.

In Washington, D.C., we visited Howard University. There, Bishop Harry Bailey joined us in our prayers, which flowed like fountains of living water. I believe strongholds were torn down as righteousness was called forth.

The next day we walked to the Capitol and held a prayer service at the Gold Room in the Sam Rayburn Building. By the Spirit, I saw the anointing of grace, strength and righteousness hovering over our national leaders. We prayed diligently for them.

At the Lincoln Memorial, we read aloud the Emancipation Proclamation and prayed that the Church be used to bring our nation together under God with liberty and justice for all. We prayed for prayer to be restored to our schools and for God to be a protective covering over our children. I sensed, and others did as well, that God was giving us an emancipator anointing.

I believe the Kettle Tour was part of God's plan for the healing of America. Thanks to the supporting prayers of hundreds of stay-at-home intercessors, we were spiritually "on target" every place our feet trod. Everywhere we went, we had signs of God's holy presence. We felt like we had been sent, as was John the Baptist, to prepare the way for revival. We sensed a shifting in the heavenly realm.

Now when He had taken the scroll, the four living creatures and the twenty-four elders fell down before the Lamb, each having a harp, and golden bowls full of incense, which are the prayers of the saints. And they sang a new song, saying: "You are worthy to take the scroll, and to open its seals; for You were slain, and have redeemed us to God by Your blood out of every tribe and tongue and people and nation, and have made us kings and priests to our God; and we shall reign on the earth."

REVELATION 5:8-10

CHAPTER 17

Glimpses from the Mountaintop

I believe that in this time, as never before, that God is wooing and drawing us—His Church—to Himself. He wants to cover us with His pinions and protect us from the plans of the enemy. As we see His purposes unfolding around us, we will draw nearer for a closer view and He will become our single focus. We will enjoy mountaintop experiences—those times when God's presence becomes divinely real to us through supernatural revelations or visitations. Then, we experience His agape love for our brothers and sisters in His Body. I believe God was revealing this in a fresh way to me one morning in the desert where I had gone with a group of believers to pray and be with Him.

One morning, each of us went to a separate place to pray and focus on Jesus. I found a large cave and walked into it. It was dark, so I was cautious about venturing very far into its corridors. I was thinking about how God hid Moses "in the cleft of the rock." Then I said, in great faith, "God, just as Moses asked You, let me see Your glory."

He did! The dark cave began to fill with light, and I was swallowed up in the beauty of the Lord. Time seemed to stand still. I began to worship and praise Him, lost in adoration. Then, as I looked back toward the entrance, I saw an angel, much larger than I, standing by a tree, holding a drawn sword. I instinctively shrank back because I never before had seen a real angel. I have often experienced their presence in the spirit realm around me, but I had never seen one as I did then.

When our group gathered later to pray, we all shared similar experiences! Another woman had seen the angel standing in the same spot. God had revealed Himself in varying ways to each of us.

Suddenly, I heard someone say, "Look up."

I had on sunglasses and a hat to block the sun, but this light was so bright that I scarcely was able to look. Then I saw, just for seconds, what looked like a throne. A rainbow began to form a circle around the throne. Then we watched as the throne disappeared and a cross began descending and stopped in front of the sun inside the rainbow. It seemed that God was smiling at us.

The next night the four of us went to the plateau, planning to make a symbolic worship offering to the Lord on behalf of the entire Body of Christ. A minister from England had given me the ancient Hebrew instructions for the wine, corn and oil mixture to use as a burnt offering to the Lord. Part of the mixture was to be placed in my best crystal bowl and the other part in a common bowl. We poured the mixture into the two containers and placed them in the fire according to the instructions.

As it was burning, a cloud of smoke began to envelop us. Each night prior to this night we had stoked the fire and had to move away as the smoke moved toward us. This night was different. The four of us stood completely encompassed in this cloud of smoke. We never stoked the fire and the fire never diminished. We recalled Scriptures about God's being "by day . . . a pillar of cloud to lead the way, and by night . . . a pillar of fire" (Exod. 13:21), leading the Israelites in the wilderness. We were standing in the midst of the smoke, but our eyes were not burning and no one was coughing. One of us spoke the Scripture, "Who is this coming up from the wilderness, leaning on [the arm of] her beloved?" (Song of Sol. 8:5). The smoke rose from around us and

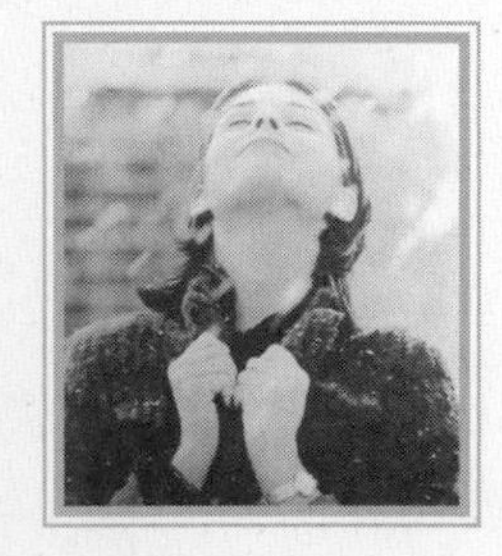

God longs for us to be one Body in Him—this has been His design from the beginning!

went heavenward. We then witnessed a display in the heavens I have never seen in my life—and I have lived many years. The display of the ensuing "fireworks" in the sky seems impossible in the natural realm. It appeared that one star would break open and become five stars, and at one point we counted 31 shooting stars in a moment. We believed this royal display in the heavens was a supernatural sign affirming the revelations we had earlier of Jesus' absolute love for His Church.

Continually during our stay in the desert, we felt God was giving us a sense of His corporate Church that He is raising up for Himself in this hour. We sensed more deeply His purpose for bringing us to this desert prayer site. As we prayed and worshipped, there was a seamless mixing of our individual anointings. He was blending our individual gifts, anointings and offerings and making us one. He was showing us in fresh ways that this is what He wants to do with His Church worldwide. He longs for us to be one Body in Him—this has been His eternal design from the beginning! He wants to bring His Church to a corporate anointing that divinely intertwines individual and corporate giftings. Why can't we see ourselves as He sees us?

Isaiah 65:8 says, "As the new wine is found in the cluster, and one says, 'Do not destroy it, for a blessing is in it,' so will I do for My servants' sake, that I may not destroy them all." I believe this cluster represents various denominations working together instead of in isolation, as we do now. Oh, that God's kingdom and dominion purposes would be fulfilled!

HEART TO HEART WITH THE FATHER

As we saw in the desert, when one prays seriously to know what's on God's heart, eventually you will be turned toward Israel. This small nation is the centerpiece in God's master plan for His earth. His plans and purposes are inextricably bound to His covenant people. Even mature intercessors are awakening to a fuller appreciation of Israel's place in God's eternal blueprint. As intercessors pray, God is giving fresh revelation of the importance of His Church knowing her identify in Israel. The divine calling on Israel, according to Genesis 12:1-3, includes being the covenant Jewish people of God, having the promised land of Israel and blessing all families of the earth.

A few months after being in the desert, I went to Israel as a delegate to the All Nations Consultation convened by Tom Hess in Jerusalem. I was there during the 10-day period known as the Days of Awe, which occurs from Rosh Hashanah through Yom Kippur. I want to share an experience I had while there.

Speakers from various nations addressed the assembly, giving us wonderful reports of God's activities in their nations. The worship was some of the holiest I have ever experienced. There were times God brought a holy hush for us to wait upon Him. During these quiet times, we sensed the Holy Spirit brooding over us. His Bride was delightfully lingering in her Bridegroom's presence. The angels of God filled the auditorium, causing the army of God to rise and battle in the heavenlies.

During the afternoon of Yom Kippur, I left the meeting room and walked outside to a garden. I sat under a tree and began to worship the Lord privately. I poured out my heart to Him, thanking Him again for all I had experienced and all He had revealed to me the past few days.

Suddenly, I had a forceful sense that God wanted to speak. As I waited silently, I began to sense the heartbeat of God talking to me about His love for His people. I have never before experienced such a flood of love. I was no longer aware of time or earthly surroundings. What seemed to be on the Father's heart that moment was His unequaled deep love and yearning for His Bride, the Church, to draw close to His Son. Oh! What causes us to resist His love and keep Him at a distance? I sensed His pain for the ways we criticize and fail to love one another.

God was speaking to me about unity or the lack of unity in the hearts of believers who want to see revival come forth. So intense was my desire to listen that I hardly dare breathe.

Then, the words from Psalm 66:18 (*NIV)*, "If I had cherished sin in my heart, the Lord would not have listened," were cleansing my own heart. I rejoice in God's absolute righteousness and perfect justice at all times regardless of my circumstances. I sensed so deeply that we must have unity of hearts among all true believers. Jesus prayed to His Father in John 17:20-23, "I do not pray for these alone, but also for those who will believe in Me through their word; that they all may be one, as You, Father, are in Me, and I in You; that they also may be one in Us, that the world may believe that You sent Me. And the glory which You gave Me I have given them, that they may be one just as We are one . . . and that the world may know that You have sent Me, and have loved them as You have loved Me."

I found myself repenting to God for my sins and praying for the entire Body of Christ. This was bigger than me. I don't quite know how to articulate what happened next. It was as though, in the spirit, I entered the heart of our Father God and felt His agonizing pain over the strife and division in His Church. The Father then reminded me of a recent incident when I spoke against a leader in the Body who was causing others pain. God shared with me that, even as I was speaking critical words, His mercy and grace were flowing to me to prevent my separation from Him. I saw my sinful condition and wept. He began to show me other areas in my life that could have separated me from Him. Out of the depth of His love, He will bring correction to our lives. Oh, the awesome mercy and grace of God!

I began weeping again, praying that His entire Church would come forth in purity, holiness and revival. I had a picture of the Bridegroom beckoning His Bride simply to Himself. I saw the heart of God that is broken when we fail to love Him and one another. I saw His heart ripped in great shreds when we criticize each other. Our cruel, careless words grieve Him.

It was not as if the ills of the world were solved in that moment. I simply saw the heart of God beating with compassion, tender love and yearning for us, and yet we, His Church, keep going our own ways. The Church is doing many good works, but God wants most of all simply to fellowship with us. His desire is that His Bride be prepared for her beloved Bridegroom. God is ravished with love for us. May we, His Church, experience His transcendent, radiant beauty and His love. May we respond to this cry of His heart.

Grow Not Weary

I thank God for the swelling tide of worldwide prayer that I've seen rising over the past three decades, and I am reminded of

Proverbs 16:15, "In the light of the king's face is life, and his favor is like a cloud of the latter rain." So be diligent seekers of the things of our God. There is a promise:

> For God is not unjust so as to forget your work and the love which you have shown toward His name, in having ministered and in still ministering to the saints. And we desire that each one of you show the same diligence so as to realize the full assurance of hope until the end, that you may not be sluggish, but imitators of those who through faith and patience inherit the promises (Heb. 6:10-12, *NASB*).

Persevering in prayer is worth the cost.

I pray that the Holy Spirit will move among us and replace our stony hearts with hearts of tenderness, kindness and compassion toward each other. I pray that we learn to persevere in the things of God, able to press near the throne in order to avail ourselves of His transforming presence.

He who sows to the Spirit will of the Spirit reap everlasting life. And let us not grow weary while doing good, for in due season we shall reap if we do not lose heart. Therefore, as we have opportunity, let us do good to all.

GALATIANS 6:8-10

EPILOGUE

Believing in Miracles

Every day, you and I live out of the wonders of God's love and compassion. We may not realize this when it is happening, but it does not stop His compassion and love from flowing to us. Perhaps you are in a place in your life where miracles don't seem possible—where God seems very far away. Take heart. Let me tell you a story of a time in my life when I was in that same place. Perhaps it will give you hope, increase your faith and lead you ever closer to the loving heart of God.

A very close friend of mine, Alice, had received a sovereign touch of healing in her life. The compassionate heart of God reached out to Alice and her family.

When we lived in Pasadena, Texas, in 1954, we met Alice and Bryant McDonald. Alice soon became my closest friend. She had a daughter a year older than my son Jim, and another daughter the same age as my son John. The year was 1959, and I was expecting our third child.

One Sunday after church, I invited the McDonald family to our home for lunch. Jim and I took the two girls and our sons home. Bryant called us about two o'clock that afternoon, advising us that Alice had started to spit up blood on their way to our house, so he had taken her to the hospital. They ran all types of tests, and a week later determined she had tuberculosis.

The doctors referred Alice to the Jewish Sanitarium for Tuberculosis in Denver, Colorado. Friends from the church helped Bryant care for the two girls. Alice had been in the hospital for three months when Janet, her seven-year-old daughter, started having the same symptoms as her mother. She also received a diagnosis of tuberculosis. Bryant flew with Janet to Denver, where she was placed in the same hospital as her mother.

One evening, Bryant called me and asked us to gather the elders of the church for prayer. He had received a report about Alice. One of her lungs had collapsed, and the other lung was deteriorating rapidly. This would require major surgery within the next few days.

At this point, I was not walking close to the Lord, but I was in church—and I loved Alice and Bryant. They were, to me, the epitome of what Christians should be; but I was not in that same place.

The elders gathered at our home, and we began praying for grace for Alice and Bryant. We asked God to give Alice the strength she needed to go through the surgery. When we had finished our prayers, one man said, "You know, God healed people when Jesus walked the face of the earth. I am going to pray and ask God to touch and heal Alice."

All of us gasped. That was beyond our comprehension of what God could or would do. We had prayed only for a skilled surgeon and for strength and grace for Alice and Bryant.

God had bigger plans.

Two days later I was standing at my kitchen window when I saw Bryant drive into our driveway. When he got out of the car, he was smiling and beaming. The thought crossed my mind that

Bryant looked drunk. As it turned out, he was high—but only on happiness.

"Bobbye, the doctor just phoned me," he said jubilantly. "They tested Alice this morning before surgery and she was totally clear. There are no symptoms or signs of tuberculosis."

When the doctor advised Alice she was free to leave, she asked, "Would you check my daughter, Janet? If Jesus healed me, I believe He will heal her, too." The doctors complied with Alice's request and discovered Janet was also free of tuberculosis.

When both of them came home four days later, it was a tremendous testimony to our church and to those who had gathered in my home on Sunday evening to pray for them.

Our families have stayed close through the years. I once explained to Alice and Bryant that they were the rock that Jesus placed in my life—a rock that I could not go over or around. Through their miraculous testimony, I knew that I needed to pursue Jesus long before I knew how.

I encourage you to believe in the miraculous for your own life. Pursue intimacy with the great Healer, the matchless Physician and see your own life transformed!

Endnotes

Introduction

1. Dick Eastman, *Love on Its Knees* (Grand Rapids, MI: Baker Book House Company, 1978), n.p.

Chapter 1

1. Francis Frangipane, "Pursuing the Stature of Christ," *Ministries of Francis Frangipane*, January 12, 2001. http://www.inchristsimage.org (accessed November 8, 2001).

Chapter 4

1. George Whitefield, quoted in William D. Blake, *Almanac of the Christian Church* (Minneapolis, MN: Bethany House, 1987), n.p.

Chapter 6

1. Tommy Tenney, *The God Chasers* (Shippensburg, PA: Destiny Image Publishers, 1998), n.p.
2. Amy Carmichael, source unknown.

Chapter 8

1. Bonnie Shannonhouse, *The Lost Coin—The Little Hours* (Annapolis, MD: Tapestry, n.d.), n.p.
2. Ibid.
3. John Calvin, quoted in Shannonhouse.
4. John Calvin, quoted in Shannonhouse.

Chapter 9

1. Cindy Jacobs, *Women of Destiny* (Ventura, CA: Regal Books, 1998), n.p.
2. Ibid.
3. Ibid.

Chapter 10

1. Jennifer Kennedy Dean, *He Leads Me Beside Still Waters* (Nashville, TN: Broadman and Holman Publishers, 2001), n.p.

Chapter 11

1. Henri J. M. Nouwen, *Life of the Beloved* (New York: The Crossroad Publishing Company, 1992), p. 30.
2. Ibid.
3. Ibid., p. 31.

Chapter 12

1. Alice Smith, U.S. Prayer Center Newsletter, July 7, 2001.

Chapter 13

1. Tommy Tenney, *God's Favorite House* (Shippensburg, PA: Destiny Image Publishers, 1999), p. 127.

Chapter 14

1. C. Austin Miles, "In the Garden" (Hall-Mack Co., 1912).

About the Author

Bobbye Byerly is a woman of enthusiasm, warmth and love for the Lord. Her strong relationship with Jesus is a testimony of God's healing power. Until 1961, when Jesus set her free, Bobbye was a woman wounded and trapped by difficult life circumstances. She explains, "He delivered me from darkness into His marvelous light. He healed me from the pain of the past by revealing to me His love, so I want to share His love with other hurting people."

Her teaching ministry has brought emotional restoration and spiritual strength to many people. Bobbye has traveled extensively throughout the United States and abroad, teaching on such subjects as:

- Knowing God and making Him known
- Intimacy with our beloved Bridegroom
- Healing family relationships

- Prayer, intercession, worship and spiritual warfare
- Choosing life by loving the Lord our God, clinging to Him and obeying Him

Bobbye currently serves on the executive board for the National Prayer Committee, the Mission America Facilitation Committee, North America United Christian Women Ministry, the U.S. Strategic Prayer Network, and Tapestry Ministry. She also serves on the International Apostolic Council and the Toward Jerusalem Council II Spiritual Unity Committee.

She served as director of prayer for the World Prayer Center for over two years and as prayer leader for AD 2000 and Beyond. She was involved in Aglow International from 1977 to 1998. Bobbye was appointed U.S. national president of Aglow International in 1993 and served in that capacity through 1997. She also served as a member on the International Board of Directors from 1983 through 1997.

Bobbye is the wife of Jim Byerly, a retired engineering consultant who is also her strongest supporter and intercessor. Bobbye and Jim are the parents of three wonderful sons and three daughters-in-love. They have four grandsons and one granddaughter.